RAMAKRISHNA
AND
THE VITALITY
OF
HINDUISM

RAMAKRISHNA
AND
THE VITALITY
OF
HINDUISM

SOLANGE LEMAITRE

Translated by Charles Lam Markmann

THE OVERLOOK PRESS
Woodstock, New York

First published in 1984 by

The Overlook Press
Lewis Hollow Road
Woodstock, New York 12498

Copyright © 1959 Editions du Seuil
First published in France by Editions de Seuil, Paris
Translated from the French Ramakrishna
et Le Vitalite du Hindouisme
Translation copyright © Longmans, Green & Co. Ltd. 1969

LIBRARY OF CONGRESS CATALOGING IN PUBLICATION DATA

Ramakrishna and the vitality of Hinduism.
(Overlook spiritual masters series: 3)
Rev. ed. of translation of: Râmakrishna et la
vitalité de l'hindouisme. 1968.
Bibliography: p.
1. Ramakrishna, 1836-1886. 2. Hindus—India—Biography.
3. Ramakrishna Mission. I. Title.
BL1280.292.R36L4513   1984
294.5'55'0924 [B]   84-5163
ISBN 0-87951-194-X

BL1280.292.R36L4513   1984   294.5'55'092 [B]   84-5163

Printed in U.S.A.

Help me to pass from nonbeing to being;
Help me to pass from darkness to light;
Help me to pass from death to immortality.

—BRIHAD-UPANISHAD, I, iii–28

Contents

अथातः पवमानानामेवाभ्यारोहः स वै खलु प्रस्तोता
साम प्रस्तौति स यत्र प्रस्तुयात्तदेतानि जपेदसतो मा सद्गमय
तमसो मा ज्योतिर्गमय मृत्योर्मामृतम् गमयेति स यदा-
हासतो मा सद्गमयेति मृत्युर्वा असत्सदमृतं मृत्योर्मामृतं
गमयामृतं मा कुर्वित्येवैतदाह तमसो मा ज्योतिर्गमयेति मृत्युर्वै
तमो ज्योतिरमृतं मृत्योर्मामृतं गमयामृतं मा कुर्वित्येवैतदाह
मृत्योर्मामृतं गमयेति नात्र तिरोहितमिवास्ति । अथ यानीत-
राणि स्तोत्राणि तेष्वात्मनेऽन्नाद्यमागायेत्तस्मादु तेषु वरं वृणीत
यं कामं कामयेत तथ्ऽस एप एवंविदुद्गातात्मने वा यज-
मानाय वा यं कामं कामयते तमागायति तद्धैतल्लोकजिदेव न
हैवालोक्यताया आशास्ति य एवमेतत्साम वेद ॥ २८ ॥ इति
तृतीयं ब्राह्मणम् ॥ ३ ॥

Introduction

Among the innumerable faces of Hindu spirituality
that have illuminated the sky of India and still illumi-
nate it, that of Sri Ramakrishna glows with splendor
all its own, like a star of the first magnitude and
remarkable mystic radiance, for in the eyes of Hindu-
ists Ramakrishna represents an *Avatar,* or Incarnation,
of the Divine.

According to Indian tradition, the gods can assume
incarnations in the persons of beings ineluctably subject to the law of *Karma,* but of their own will, in
order to fulfill a task deemed necessary at a given time,
including the mission of succoring mankind in distress
or that of reviving faith when it tends to diminish.
These Divine Incarnations, whether limited or total, the
number of which cannot be restricted, are called *Avatara,* or Descents. To *Brahman* (the Divine), Rama-

krishna asserted, each of them is what the wave is to the ocean.

The Hindu god (one of the *Trimurti,* or Trinity) who is most often incarnated, Vishnu who became Krishna, the god with the universal soul, confesses himself in these terms to Arjuna in the *Bhagavad-Gita:*

> Even though I am the soul without beginning or end, imperishable, even though I am the Lord of all creatures, I am born of my own power by virtue of my own nature. Whenever the order of the world trembles and disorder threatens, I produce myself. My birth, like my work, is divine. He who knows this in all truth does not go to a new birth when he throws off his mortal body—he comes to me, Arjuna. (*Bhagavad-Gita,* French translation by E. Senart, page 69.)

Regarded by the greatest theologians of his time, who saw in him the essential revealing signs of the Descent of the Divine, as a Divine Incarnation—the incarnation of Krishna, according to Vivekananda, his spiritual son—Ramakrishna demonstrated a religious vocation, at once glorious and precocious, from his earliest childhood. It was an apparently ordinary existence, devoid of incident but accompanied by an intense inner life, in which his sublime destiny was to be developed to its final achievement. The spiritual ascent accomplished by the saint of Dakshineswar through a series of remarkable mystic experiences still amazes and stirs the world to which, moreover, he set the example of universal love and universal understanding

Sri Ramakrishna

of all religions. He was truly the incarnation of the
eternal spiritual message that has been whispered
through the millennia by India: "Truth is One but the
Wise have given it different names." (*Rig-Veda.*)

Almost a contemporary branch (he lived in the
nineteenth century) growing out of the vast trunk of
the *Veda* that has overshadowed India since the very
beginning of the age of its spiritual flowering—its
inexhaustible sap has fed the Indian soul—Sri Rama-

❀

krishna, in truth a golden branch of the Vedic ideal, is one of its purest, its most dazzling personifications.

This "madman of God," as he was called, who lived at the same time in heaven and on earth—he spent half his life in ecstasy—illuminated Bengal with his experiences and his expressions of perfect faith in a single God with many names who can take on all forms and remain without any form.

We are indebted to Romain Rolland, and the magnificent book that he devoted to Ramakrishna some thirty years ago, for the revelation of the saint to France and indeed to Europe, where he had been known to only a limited audience. The success of this book was considerable. Since its publication the Hindu saint has gone unceasingly forward to new conquests, for Romain Rolland's book still arouses the same enthusiasm in later generations. The double publication of *The Life of Ramakrishna* and the same author's *Life of Vivekananda,* which is its continuation, has formed a lasting link between the Orient and the Occident, a link augmented by all those others that are constantly being forged. At the present time the exchanges and the bonds between the two continents, which are increasing at a more rapid pace, are bringing to fruition the desire of so many minds and of Rolland's in particular: to bring the men of Asia and Europe closer in a mutual understanding.

"The visible God who leads His elect to the invisible God . . ." (Ramakrishna)

There is so rich a bibliography on the illustrious saint, there have been so many books published in India, in Europe, and in America, that it would be out of the question to read them all. Some are inaccessible by reason of their language—Bengali—or their un-availability on the market. But the whole of the origi-nal and translated works that are within our reach, the list of which is far too long to be set forth here, is enough to make it possible for us to know many of the aspects of the priest of Dakshineswar. He had count-less faces; and so it might be said that no book devoted to Ramakrishna is unimportant: each has its value and represents a stone in the edifice erected to his memory.

The Gospel of Ramakrishna, priceless among all these sources of information, was the work of Mahendra Nath Gupta, the intimate and devoted disciple of the worshiper of Kali. The director of an educational institution in Calcutta, a modest, reserved man, Mahendra refused to sign this invaluable *Gospel* with anything but the pseudonym of an initial: M. For many years, until his Master's death, he recorded al-most daily the conversations between Ramakrishna and his intimates or his foreign visitors, as well as the important and the insignificant changes and incidents, the theater of which was the monastery. This disciple, M., left five volumes in Bengali, of which the first was translated in 1897 and the last in 1932, after its author's death.

One cannot even mention the name of Mahendra Nath Gupta without expressing profound gratitude for

his devotion to his *guru* and for the service that he
rendered to his memory and his worshipers by describ-
ing in his notes, all taken from life, what that daily life
was like in the garden-temple of Dakshineswar; and
above all by illuminating a large part of Ramakrishna's
thought at a time when, having attained its full matu-
rity, it was expressed in all its plenitude.

The great Hindu saint did not write. He was content
to speak to those who went to visit him. Through *The
Gospel of M.* we learn that, even though the Master
scaled the highest peaks of metaphysical speculation
with some of his visitors, he did not hesitate to descend
to the humblest concerns of day-to-day existence, to
which he contributed an unexpected feeling for the
practical. His remarks were often seasoned with a sense
of humor. How many times his historian concludes an
episode with the same words: "And then everyone
laughed."

To this *Gospel,* and to the excellent biography by
Swami Nikhilananda that preceded it, we are indebted
for many of the sayings and events that are retold in
this book.

Vivekananda's contribution to the records concerning his Master is of course of the first importance.
Ramakrishna's dearest and closest disciple—he completed his *guru's* mission by spreading his spiritual
message throughout the world—Vivekananda has
written pages on the saint that are eloquent in their
fervor.

Among those who were with Ramakrishna until the

end, Swami Brahmananda, his next favorite disciple after Vivekananda, survived his Master until 1922. He constitutes a source of direct information by reason of his writings: *A Monastic Discipline,* a work of great scope because of its teaching, which is a reflection of Ramakrishna's, and a smaller book, *The Sayings of His Guru,* which is of all the greater worth because Swami Brahmananda enjoyed the inestimable privilege of the closest participation in his Master's daily life. Ramakrishna believed that Rakhal (who was to become Swami Brahmananda later) had been one of the playmates of Krishna—in other words, one of his own playmates in an earlier life.

In addition to these written sources, the oral tradition taught and lived in the *ashram* or *math* consecrated to the Order of the Ramakrishna Mission—whether in India, in America, or in Gretz, near Paris—affords other sources of information on the message of the priest of Dakshineswar.

In the *ashram* at Gretz, founded and directed by Swami Siddheswarananda, who had been ordained a monk of the Order of Ramakrishna by Swami Brahmananda himself, the Master's own disciple, the teaching is carried on with vitality and richness. It is saddened only by the painful loss of Swami Siddheswarananda, who died of illness on April 2, 1957. Friendly contacts with him during the years of his ministry at the *ashram* of Gretz gave me the opportunity for long conversations with him about Ramakrishna. I should like now to express my thanks to him and my devotion to his memory. Swami Siddheswarananda was a great and worthy successor to his Master.

In spite of all the information available, in spite of all the zeal with which one strives in one's own turn to pay a tribute of admiration to the remarkable personality of the great Hindu saint, one is filled with a genuine sense of impotence before the task of painting a portrait that no frame can enclose. Such is sometimes the case with certain men who have left the stage of this world and perhaps too with others who are still among us. In the case of Ramakrishna the difficulty is much greater.

This remarkable man is beyond the reach of any attempt at synthesis, as one examines him more deeply, because of his many contradictory aspects—or aspects that seem to be contradictory because of their rich complexity which he himself was so marvelously able to unify. He had every talent. Beneath an outer comportment that never varied, that was extreme in its simplicity, he was as mobile as the sea, as burning as fire, as pure as a child, but with the experience of a man without age, a man already established in eternity.

His disciples have confessed their incapacity to know their *guru* in depth. How would it be possible to grasp the thousand-faceted spirit of Ramakrishna? How would it be possible to define this man who called himself ignorant and who knew all though he had learned nothing, who answered the most puzzling

questions with a competence and a wisdom that filled
the most eminent theologians with amazement? He
was a man of prodigy and mystery.

This book does not pretend to be an exhaustive study
of the priest of Dakshineswar and his teaching drawn
from the examination of the innumerable works already published. My goal is simply to try to give some
new sense of his love of God, that *Bhakti* that made
him sing divine praises all through the day, that *Bhakti*
that, he declared, was his sole reason for being.

RAMAKRISHNA
AND
THE VITALITY
OF
HINDUISM

1

The Hindu Tradition

The *Vedas*

Perhaps, before embarking on the story of Rama-krishna, it would be advisable to sum up briefly the major elements of the religion that shaped him.

This man of the summits was born in a country—India—that owes the deeply religious character of its civilization to the Divine Revelation that was received at the dawn of the ages by inspired wise men endowed with supernatural intuition, the *Rishis,* who transcribed this revelation into the *Vedas,* or Holy Scriptures.

The content of the Vedic scriptures is regarded by the adepts of the Hindu religion as the fruit of a direct verbalization, or *sruti,* which came from *Brahman* and was expressed by *Brahman* in the form of words embodying the eternal Truth. This eternal Truth cannot change; it is the sacred Knowledge (*Veda* means "Knowledge") that was to dominate the whole religious, moral, and social life of India from the beginning of time until today by the permanence of its tradition throughout the development of the sects to which it was to give birth and by whatever name it might be given. It is a rare occurrence in the history of mankind to find such a continuity underlying the development of a civilization.

Since India is a country of vast territory and a great variety of peoples, with diverse races and languages, certain variations arose during the centuries in the interpretation of the Vedic Texts of the Revelation, without causing any modification in the essence of the tradition. Sects came into being. Hence there exists in India not one sole religion but a cluster of related religions all born of a common source, the *Veda,* which stands for orthodoxy in the eyes of all of them. These various sects, which are designated by the name of *Sanatana-Dharma* in India and which are called Hinduism in Europe, do not imply—and this is remarkable —any conflict among their followers.

The *Vedas,* or Sacred Books, the bearers of the traditional doctrine, form a large collection of documents, only part of which is known to us; and even this is only partly accessible to Western mentalities, so removed from Hindu conceptions.

What is found in the *Rig-Veda,* the first of the Vedic Books, has no equivalent anywhere in the religious history of mankind. A philosophic teaching of lofty range is expressed in hymns of exceptional poetry, powerful in their lyricism and often and deliberately in their symbolism, it seems, for the secret of the *Veda* must remain impenetrable to the profane. According to the Sages, these are mysteries whose origin is not human. The hidden meanings of visible things should belong only to him who has the capacity to sense them beneath appearances, to the initiate.

The *Vedas* are the oldest documents that the world knows, because they date back to the prehistoric period that is lost in the night of time. They have bestowed on man the concept of the Absolute that has always been and still remains the basic attitude, at once religious and metaphysical, of Indian thought. The Vedic Revelation proclaimed UNITY. This concept of the One without another, once it has been created, always mandatorily identical to itself, whence multiplicity has sprung, gave India her religious basis at the same time as Hindu Unity, purely traditional in its nature, which needs for its preservation no support other than its own doctrine.

The hymns of the *Rig-Veda* place us face to face

FOLLOWING PAGES Episodes from the *Mahabharata* (Ellora, ninth century)

❁

5

with the man who seeks to resolve the enigma of the world, and also with the man who prays, who adores.

There was neither being nor nonbeing, there was neither the atmosphere nor the sky above. What moves? In what direction, under whose keeping?

Nor was there death then, nor immortality. Day was not separate from night. Only the One breathed, without an alien breath, of Himself—and there was nothing other than He.

Whence did this creation come—whether it was created or not created? He whose eye watches over it from the summit of heaven, He alone knows; and does even He know it? (*Rig-Veda,* X.)

This metaphysical question is answered by another hymn:

He who gives life, He who gives strength, He whose commandments are revered by all the gods, whose shadow is immortality, whose shadow is death—what is this God that we should honor Him with sacrifices?

He by whom the mountains of snow have their existence—and the sea with the distant river—He whose arm is the regions of the sky—who is this God that we should honor Him with sacrifices?

He by whom space is made splendid and earth is made solid—by whom the sky, even the summit of the sky, was erected—He who has measured the realms of the ether—who is this God that we should honor Him with sacrifices? (*Rig-Veda,* X.)

This *Rig-Veda,* the most ancient and the most important of the four *Vedas*, contains a thousand hymns that are prayers or praises addressed to the gods, above all to the primordial God, the Creator. Their sonority gives these hymns a magic power when they are chanted according to rigid rules that make it possible for the officiants to enter into relations with "the essence of things."

In his *Gospel* Mahendra Nath Gupta tells of the chants to which, outside the regular hours of worship, Ramakrishna and his disciples in the monastery of Dakshineswar devoted themselves many times during every day, sometimes with no other reason than their joy in singing and dancing out of love for the Divine, in a spontaneous testimony.

The *Upanishads*

Among the Sacred Texts we must include the *Upanishads,* esoteric philosophical treatises of major importance. They set forth the great principles of universal metaphysics in the guise of fables or poems of cosmic inspiration. They reflect a pure monism, seeking Unity in the heart of diversity, elaborating on the theme of *atman-Brahman.* The credo of the *Upanishads,* the famous *tat tvam asi,* means: "You are It." *It* is the Absolute, *Brahman*; a word that overwhelms with the virtues that it embraces.

❋

It would be impossible to understand Ramakrishna, who was nurtured on the *Upanishads,* without knowing what is meant by *Brahman* and *atman.*

Transcendent, immanent, beyond all distinction, *Brahman* can be grasped only by the spirit, for it incarnates the Supreme Divinity, but every creature has within himself a spark of *Brahman-atman.* This *atman* that no one can impair, that is immutable and eternal, should not be confused with the personal self. It is part of *Brahman,* as is salt dissolved in salt water. Whatever is is *Brahman,* or the Sacred Word, which cannot be defined. It has neither condition nor qualification. *Brahman* can be compared to the universal soul "that contains all individual souls as the ocean contains all the drops of water of which it is composed." (*Brihad-Upanishad.*)

Atman, which is a spark of Divinity—of *Brahman*—can be defined only by negatives: intangible, it cannot be apprehended; indestructible, it cannot be destroyed; without bonds, it cannot be bound to anything, and so forth.

Smaller than the smallest, larger than the largest, *atman* lies hidden in every creature's heart, The wise man, released from desire, whose senses are allayed, knows in himself the majesty of *atman.* Immobile, *atman* journeys afar; without moving it travels through space. The grief of the wise man ends as soon as he grasps the vast *atman,*

Kirtan chant at Hardwar

11

The wise man released from desire (Kashmir)

which penetrates everywhere, bodiless in the midst of the body, stable within the transitory. This *atman* cannot be arrived at by study or by science; it is by *atman* itself that *atman* can be known. Then the wise man's *atman* recognizes its own essence. (*Kathaka-Upanishad*, I, ii, 20–23.)

It is through meditation, mental concentration, and *Yoga* that one attains to this *atman*, this Self-in-Itself that is far beyond human consciousness. Once relieved of its fleshly envelope, *atman* fuses into *Brahman*, for it is identical with *Brahman*.

The purpose of the Hindu religion is to achieve the identity of *atman* and *Brahman*, to accomplish their fusion and thus to break the *samsara*, or cycle of rebirths.

"As thousands of sparks identical in their nature burst forth from a fire, so the innumerable creatures emerge from the indestructible Being and return to it." (*Mundaka-Upanishad,* II, i, i.)

The *Bhagavad-Gita*

It is this return to the original source that the Hindu tradition preaches in its Sacred Books through the teachings of the various philosophical systems. It is the quest for Deliverance: the *Moksha,* through the fusion of the Self with the universal that constitutes the central theme of the *Bhagavad-Gita,* or *Song of the Lord,* that universally known epic poem wholly steeped in mystic fervor. A fragment of the *Mahabharata* with its one hundred thousand strophes, it combines in its own verses religious and warrior legends mingled with philosophical concepts, stated in a magnificent lyric poetry like that already produced by the Vedic hymns.

The *Gita* preaches total union, *Bhakti* in the Unique Being of the countless Names who is incarnated by Krishna in the poem to pour out the treasures of his thought to Arjuna, who harkens to him before going into battle. As between the two speculative systems that it expounds, monism and dualism, the *Gita* adopts no special doctrine with definite dogmas; rather, it represents a religious orientation that remains within the

❁

Hindu tradition. Above all it represents passionately mystic faith, infinite devotion to the Lord, that *Bhakti* that Krishna put into these words in the *Gita:*

> He who sees me in everything and who sees everything in me is never separated from me, and I am never separated from him. He who at the hour of his end rejects his mortal envelope while thinking solely of me rejoins my being: of this there can be no doubt.

While the *Mahabharata* has rightly been regarded as a peak of Hinduism—it has been called the fifth *Veda*—the *Bhagavad-Gita* is invested with the dignity of a kind of *Gospel* (Renou); therefore it is deemed by special grace to be a *Sruti*.

The *Upanishads* express the greatest of human anxieties in metaphors. Based on the orthodoxy of the *Veda* in their teaching, they carry farther the earlier speculations, particularly in defining the theme of *atman-Brahman,* or the relation between the individual and the universal souls.

The *Darçanas* and *Yoga*

Among the Hindus, religion and philosophy represent the two inseparable sides of a single tradition. Speculation ranges unceasingly, but the various metaphysical and cosmological conceptions of India are not divergent doctrines; rather they are developments of

Patanjali

the same doctrine according to certain "points of view," in directions that differ but are in no way incompatible with one another. The Sanskrit word *darçana* means, precisely, "point of view." It denotes each of these conceptions that together start from a common source, the *Veda*.

The authors of the *darçanas* were ardent believers, concerned only with preserving the purity of the Vedic tradition. The orthodox *darçanas,* of which there are six, complement one another and constitute a finished picture of the universe. They were already in being in Vedic times, but they were developed principally during the age of the *Vedanta*. Two of them must be mentioned here in order to better follow Ramakrishna's religious growth.

The first with which we are concerned here is the fourth *darçana, Yoga,* which means "union" in Sanskrit, and which today is the subject of an almost excessive curiosity in the interpretation that is given to it. In fact it represents a philosophical system that denotes chiefly the efficacious union of the human being with the universal on the basis of certain age-old precepts.

The word appears for the first time in the *Katha-Upanishad*: "When the five modes of knowledge by thought are at rest and reason no longer stirs, this is what is called the supreme path. It is known by the name of *Yoga*." (VI, 10, Renou's translation.)

The word *Yoga* is equally applicable to a *darçana* whose composition in *sutras* is attributed to Patanjali.

❊

Public reading of the *Bhagavad-Gita* (Rishikesh, Himalaya)

This *Yoga,* which is a special asceticism, accepts a personal god, Isvara, and traditionally implies the union of the finite (*jivatman*) and the infinite (*Paratman*)—in other terms, the absolute fusion of the individual in the universal. *Yoga* training is preparation for the journey that leads to spiritual enlightenment. It is a part of every religious discipline in India.

The *Vedanta*

On the other hand, the *Vedanta,* which is the last of the six orthodox *darçanas,* is a sequel to the *Upanishads,* which in their turn represent the conclusion of the Vedic Texts. The *Upanishads* are the foundation of which the *Vedanta* is the completion and the crown.

The major teachings of the *Vedanta* have been gathered into a collection of "Aphorisms," to which the name of *Brahmasutras* has been given. But the most famous of the commentaries to which the *Brahmasutras* have given rise are those of Sankara, the very great Sage, who is often called Sankarasarya.

A true doctrine of pure metaphysics, one of the most tremendous philosophical conceptions to which the mind of man has risen, the *Vedanta* opens unlimited possibilities for the speculations of the spirit. It is not a closed system; quite the contrary. Its perspectives range through the Universal and the Infinite. The basis of the doctrine is still the concept of Unity, the Unity of spiritual reality, and the relations between the Supreme Self, or *Brahman,* and the individual self, or *atman.*

The path of Knowledge taught in the *Upanishads* can be summarized in this fashion:

"*Atman* is *Brahman.*"

"*So'ham:* I am he."

"*Tat tvam asi:* You yourself are It."

Potentially this formula contains all the developments of Hindu philosophy. The great *mantra* set forth by Sankara—*tat tvam asi:* "You are It"—constitutes the credo of his *advaita* (nondualism). Later it was to become that of Ramakrishna, who would unceasingly reiterate it to his disciples: "Only the ONE exists." The visible world is an illusion, an empirical reality. Sri Ramakrishna also said: "If we live in God, the visible disappears; if we live in the world, God no longer exists." This was precisely what Sankara had asserted many centuries earlier.

This does not mean that the *jiva,* the individual soul, is the peer of *Brahman,* the universal soul, for the part cannot possibly be regarded as the equivalent of the whole. But the substratum that exists in the *jiva* and in the universe is everywhere the same; this is the revelation of the ontological aspect that makes it possible to see "the real within the real."

Sankara's conclusion is this:

Since everything proceeds from the Self, since everything is resolved in the Self, and since, in the intermediate phase of preservation, everything remains steeped in the Self, for this reason it would be impossible for the Self to be perceived by any but Itself, and, consequently, everything is the Self. (Commentaries of Sri Sankarasarya, quoted by Swami Siddheswarananda in *Essay on Hindu Metaphysics,* page 66.)

The Path of Liberation represented by the *Vedanta* leads to the Realization of the Absolute. Now, Ramakrishna, and he alone, really lived the whole gamut of the *Vedanta,* which embraces the three ways of binding oneself to Reality. The first attitude illustrates the dualist position, the second modified dualism, and the third that of *advaita,* or nondualism, which was the peak of his spiritual accomplishment.

Let us say once more that *Brahman,* the Absolute that cannot be defined, "the dazzling light of lights," contained within its "scabbard of gold," through which the mind thinks but which no man can conceive, remains incommunicable.

"You ask what is *Brahman?* It is your own *atman,* which is within everything." (*Brihad-Upanishad.*) *Brahman* is pure existence; *sat* is pure intelligence; *chit* is pure beatitude: *ananda.* It is *Satchitananda.*

Inasmuch as it is impossible to conceive It in Its Totality and in Its Truth, the Hindus try to find It in Its Divine Manifestations. To adore *Brahman* in Its Attributes is to cause It to descend to the human level. Then *Brahman* assumes the guise of a personal god. It can be envisaged in any of Its Functions or Its Powers. *Brah-*

❋

man, even while It is One in Its Essence, bears innumerable names because It wears innumerable aspects, which are modalities of limitless *Brahman* in all Its Forms.

These Divine Manifestations correspond to the affinities of the believers. Their multiplicity is the more astonishing to the Western mind because each personified god may have many names, according as he may be invoked under one of his activities or under some other quality that is characteristic of him. The worshiper calls the god whom he selects his *ishta.* It is to him that the believer addresses his prayers and his chaplets, and it is through the *ishta* that the believer draws closer to *Brahman,* the Supreme Divinity for whom the gods are only intermediaries. *Brahman* contains *all* the *ishtas.* It is always *Brahman* because *everything* is *Brahman.*

Indeed, the gods can personify nature as well as Felicity, Mercy, or Death. These individualizations are merely *Brahman* as conceived by the devout, as Vishnu demonstrated when he told Siva in the the *Vishnu-Purana:* "Those who are the prey of ignorance regard me as distinct from you."

In the highly elaborate and extremely complicated mythology of the *Veda,* the divine Trinity, or *Trimurti,* dominates the multiple divine forms. It is composed of three gods who share the fundamental activities of Isvara, the generic name of the single and supreme God, the will of power, symbolizing *Brah-*

man, neuter and unknowable, and above the Trinity.

It is Brahma, who must not be confused with the impersonal *Brahman,* who possesses the power of creating; that of preserving is held by Vishnu; and, finally, the power of destruction belongs to Siva. These gods, who represent the three aspects of Isvara, constitute the great *Trimurti* whose action corresponds to the rhythm of the creation of the world: the beginning of a cycle, its complete manifestation, and its conclusion, or reabsorption into *Brahman,* the *Pralaya,* the period that precedes the next era.

Not all the Vedic gods can be mentioned here because they are beyond number, but, among those who in Hindu tradition were substituted for or added to those of the *Veda,* Brahma remains quite abstract in spite of his function as the creator. It is he who brings into being *diversity in Unity.* There is no special form of worship of him, and his shrines are rare. *Sarasvati* is the *sakti* of Brahma. *Sakti* is the word for the energy that emanates from the god and that complements him in the feminine form of a goddess.

Vishnu presides over human destinies by playing the beneficent part of the preserver of the cosmos. A god of solar origin whose cult, Vishnuism, is extremely popular, he is honored by a great number of shrines. The *sakti* of Vishnu, who is venerated on a very lofty

Brahma, master of creation, order, and revelation

Vishnu. Carried on the cosmic waters by the serpent, he dreams the world

Siva. He dances his dance of destruction and liberation

level because he is the incarnation of Divine Love, is Lakshmi, the symbol of the model wife.

The third god in the *Trimurti,* Siva, is a complex and ambivalent deity, at once beneficent and dreadful. Assuming the role of the destroyer of the universe, he annihilates in order to rebuild. He destroys the multiplicity that is the created world in order to re-create Unity. Like Kala, time, he builds and destroys without rest. The potent god of procreation, he is above all the Mahadeva, the great ascetic god of the yogis, their guide and their model because he leads them into awareness of Unity.

Siva's shrines, which are very many, are celebrated throughout the world. The most important of his *saktis*—he has many of them—is Durga, or Kali, the Terrible, the feminine, maternal aspect of god, who incarnates a splendid energy and does not destroy, like her husband, Siva, except in order to release the spirituality that exists in every being. Then, having accomplished her task, she becomes calm and gentle.

This Kali was to be selected by Ramakrishna as his preferred divinity, his Divine Mother, his *ishta,* the adoration of his life, who was to become the center of his spiritual experiences by aiding him to attain to the highest state of *samadhi,* union with God, a condition from which, as a general rule, no one returns.

Temple of Siva at Bhuwaneswar, ninth century (Orissa)

Siva and His *Sakti*

The Creation

By way of completing this short summary of the very general but basic ideas, at once religious and metaphysical, of the Hindu religion, it is worthwhile to give some attention to the process of the Creation as it is conceived in the *Sanatana-Dharma*.

It might be said that Hindu metaphysics is founded wholly on the conception of a Unique substance that is moved by a Unique rhythm with predetermined harmonies. This is the explanation of the theory of the macrocosm and the microcosm—that is, the human organism bound by a series of similarities to the outer world, the cosmos. The body is analogous to the earth, language to fire, breath to air, etc.

The rhythm of life and death is analogous to the great rhythm of the universal manifestation of *Brahman* and of universal dissolution, or cosmic sleep, *Pralaya.* Creation is only a transition from the unmanifested to the manifested, from the multiple to the One.

It is in a single inhalation that *Brahman* creates the universe and by a single exhalation that it annihilates it by reabsorbing it into itself. *Brahman* breathes eternally, creating and destroying without interrupting the continuity of the universe, the cosmos, space without boundaries.

The point of departure of the Creation is presented under the aspect of "nonknowledge or ignorance," an eternal, unmanifested substratum. Subsequently the essence of the ego appears and becomes the consciousness of the individual self and finally a material, imponderable continuum, the *pradhana* that covers space and bears within itself three *gunas.* These *gunas* are characteristics of the primordial substance. The first is *sattva,* the principle of light; the second is *rajas,* the principle of feeling; and the third is *tamas,* the principle of darkness.

The *akasa,* or ether, the material continuum, which

❊

is of exceptional fineness, gives birth to the four elements: air, fire, water, and earth. From their combination Life is born, constituting *the egg of Brahman*. This is the mixture of the three *gunas* and the four elements, including the *akasa,* that shapes the world of phenomena. This mixture creates bodies of greater and greater density. The *sattva* directs the soul toward *Brahman,* whereas the *rajas* and the *tamas* turn it in other directions. The *gunas* are the factors of the unequal aspects of human activity, the World of Names and Forms, but *everything* is *Brahman,* is part of it. The world is *Brahman* but *Brahman* is the *atman* of the universe.

Brahman is not manifested in the earliest age when the World of Names and Forms, still only potential, is sleeping. *Brahman* is the Cause. In the second period, it is manifested *Brahman,* Effect, and this interplay of Causes and Effects, of *Purusha* and *Prakriti,* is nothing more than cosmic action. Manifested and unmanifested *Brahman* alternate in eternity. *Pralaya,* or universal dissolution, makes it legitimate to say that all effects are unreal because they are reabsorbed into their causes.

The power that acts in the *akasa* is *prana,* or energy. In the Hindu concept, matter is only energy in movement, energy that differentiates itself. Everything develops into man, the turning point of the process of becoming. Man can emancipate himself from the cycle of rebirths, or *samsara,* when he has understood the illusory nature of matter. He discovers that he has

❀

emanated from *Brahman* and he strives to return to it.

This illusory matter is called *Maya*. This virtually untranslatable word does not mean *illusion*. It is, rather, phenomenon in relation to noumenon, the veil that conceals Absolute Reality, the hidden spring that forces mankind to transform itself for the Glory of the Divine.

Each period between two successive creations is called a *Kalpa,* or "day of *Brahman,*" which is the equivalent of 4.32 billion years.

> When the world perishes at the end of two *Brahmanic* periods, the *Bhavata* says, when the coarse elements enter into the original element, when the past returns under the pressure of time that has not yet begun, then you (Vishnu) remain alone under the name of Gesha. (Renou, *Hinduism*.)

Karma

The evolutionary curve of mankind corresponds to the evolutionary curve of every creature. Here again is the law of the macrocosm and the microcosm. The idea of *Karma,* the principle of causality that governs human destinies, is a central dogma of Hinduism, or *Sanatana-Dharma*. Every act, every thought produces a good or evil result, the responsibility for which will have to be met one day in this life or in another. The

❈

sum total of these effects over a whole existence represents each person's *karma.* No one can evade this law
of *Karma,* or retribution for one's actions, which ex-
plains and justifies the consequences of our thoughts
and our deeds.

Each person's current life, conditioned by the life
that preceded it, conditions his ensuing life in turn.
Consciousness, which is karmic memory, contains the
higher conscious spirit, *Vijnana,* the Divine Spark,
which in a certain fashion and to a degree may be
regarded as a "descent of the Infinite" into the apparent finite of name and form.

The gravity of suicide becomes clear under this law.
It is a refusal to live, whereas on the contrary one must
be ready to *pay* all the debts that one has contracted
through earlier actions in order to exhaust one's *karma*
and escape from *samsara,* or the cycle of rebirths.

The law of *Karma* inevitably sires the law of re-
incarnation as a necessity, because the soul is summoned to return in order to "discharge" its *karma* on
earth. According to Vedic conceptions, the soul is born
and dies very many times. It assumes temporary
"sheaths" (*koshas*), or habitations. The *Bhagavad-Gita*
(II, 22) says: "The soul incarnate throws off the old
bodies and takes on new ones as a man changes a worn
garment for another."

The *Samsara*

The life of any individual is only one life among innumerable lives, one bringing about the next and fixing the conditions that make it possible to nullify the previous *karma*. The *samsara* is only the chain of successive existences. Since the soul cannot perish like the body, it justifies the law of *Karma* by being reborn: "Every action bears its fruit, none can be annulled." To the objection that might be raised, Sankara replied:

> Since the *samsara* knows no beginning, the workings and the inequality of creation are to one another, in the relation between cause and effect, what the seed and the plant are to each other.

Sankara concludes that everything is founded on *Brahman:*

> For the individual soul, which nonknowledge renders incapable of differentiating itself from the aggregate of acts and organs, and which is blinded by the darkness of ignorance, the *samsara* in which it appears as active and passive is established by the permission of the Supreme Being, the custodian of all actions, the witness who lives within all beings, the source of all spirituality; and in consequence we have to admit that it is by its grace that we acquire Knowledge and, through Knowledge, *Moksha,* or Deliverance. The Scriptures affirm this: *Brahman* is the agent of Cause, or the First Cause in the height of action.

❀

Avatara of Vishnu (popular modern statuettes). In order to preserve or restore *dharma* on earth, Vishnu has incarnated himself particularly in . . . Matsya (the fish), Kurma (the tortoise), Varaha (the wild boar), Nara-Simba (the lion-man), Vamana (the dwarf), Parasu-Rama (Rama with ax), Ramachandra (the hero of the Ramayana), Krishna

Dharma

In order to put an end to one's *karma,* one must create no new one. But every thought adds to it. Krishna, the Divine Incarnation, offers a way out of this terrifying prospect. He declares that one stops creating *karma* from the moment when one offers up all one's actions, all one's words, all one's thoughts to the Divine.

In order that the Divine may function, one must also eliminate personal tastes and obey the Supreme Will. This continuous effort is called *dharma.*

A fundamental concept, *dharma* (the very name of the Hindu religion, *Sanatana-Dharma,* means eternal *dharma*) represents religious obligation at the same time as the pure notion of *individual duty.* Closely bound to *karma, dharma* is in some way the "support" of beings and things, the law of order extended to the ultimate degree.

The *Guru*

The universe is founded on cosmic *dharma* and every man should obey his individual *dharma.* Each has his own, which it is his business to discern in the variety of rules of conduct with which he is confronted.

❋

Each individual should choose those that are applicable to his own ineluctable inner law. The Brahmin does not have the same *dharma* as the *kshatriya*. Nor is anyone made to endure tests that exceed his powers. Here, providentially, the *guru* comes into the Hindu religion; the spiritual master who exists to offer potent assistance to his *chela,* or disciple, when the latter needs it. The *guru* can direct his *chela* toward the state of *jivan-mukti* (liberated living) if the disciple is ready, if at last his spirit is ripe.

This concept of the spiritual master, the *guru,* is peculiarly Hindu. We shall see that the acquaintance and the influence of two *gurus* in his youth were to make a profound impression on Ramakrishna's spiritual ascent by preparing his state of *jivan-mukti,* Deliverance, the basic goal of the Hindu religion. For Deliverance is nothing other than the certainty that spiritual experience will lead to the identity of the individual soul and *Brahman.*

Many avenues lead to Deliverance—"that of acts" (rituals, pilgrimages, prayers), "that of initiation," or "the path of Knowledge," which consists in *seeing* Truth. It is illumination that leads to ecstasy. Alongside these avenues, progressively developed practical methods of spiritual discipline are grouped under the name of *Yoga.*

A *yogi* (detail from the Descent of the Ganges—Mavalipuram)

Yoga

This is a matter of a collection of very ancient disciplines that assume various forms in which the technical and psychic part fulfills an important function. These diverse ascetic theories, some of which, perhaps, derive more from the search for salvation than from philosophy, have been assembled into an orthodox *darçana, Yoga,* or the philosophical system complementary to *Sankhya.* The subject is too broad to be dealt with here. Among the different roads that are

❊

represented by the *yogas,* that of devotion, religion, love was, among others, the path chosen by Rama- krishna; but this did not prevent him from practicing *Jnana-Yoga* because the purpose of the asceticism of *Jnana-Yoga* is the gaining of Knowledge, of access to noumenal Truth, to which the priest of Dakshineswar so swiftly attained. Vivekananda said of him: "He was all *Bhakti* on the outside and all *Jnana* on the inside." *Jnana-Yoga* is the most arduous road of all. One of the most striking aspects of Ramakrishna, indeed, consists in the plurality of his experiences and the rapidity of the results that he obtained from the spiritual point of view; for, even while he continued to live on the relative plane, he hardly left the Absolute.

A Thought

The Divine Being who thrusts ahead when we awaken and who falls back when we sleep, she who travels far, the unique light of lights, Thought: may what she conceives be propitious for me!

She through whom the wise, those adept laborers, achieve their mission in sacrifice and ritual—unprecedented miracle housed in our being, Thought: may what she conceives be propitious for me!

She who enwraps all that was and is and will be, the im- mortal through whom the sacrifice is offered with the

❁

seven celebrants, Thought: may what she conceives be
propitious for me!

She from whom strophes, melodies, and phrases radiate as
the spokes from the hub of the wheel, she in whom is
woven all the meditation of all creatures, Thought: may
what she conceives be propitious for me!

She who, as a good coachman guides his team, powerfully
leads men with her reins as if they were race-horses—
firm in the heart yet moving and infinitely swift,
Thought: may what she conceives be propitious for me!
(*Vajasaneyisamhita in the Yajurveda,* XXXIV, 1–6.)*

* From Renou's French translation of *Hymns and Prayers of
the Veda.*

Apsara, a heavenly nymph (Kajuharo)

41

2

The Life of Ramakrishna

Youth

It was in a period not too remote from our own—in 1836—that Ramakrishna was born in a little Bengali village sheltered by banyan trees and mangoes and surrounded by rice fields and pools: Kamarpukur.

Ramakrishna's parents, Khudiram Chattopadhyaya and Chandra Devi, who had married in 1799, were a Brahmin couple, pious and of modest means, and had lived first in Dereypore, another village nearby, which

❀

was the ancestral home of Ramakrishna's father. Their first two children were a boy, Ramkumar, born in 1805, and a girl, Katyayayani, born in 1810. As a consequence of a dispute with the rather unprincipled landowner for whom he worked, Khudiram, who had been stripped of all that he owned because he refused to bear false witness against a neighbor, decided to leave the village and establish himself in Kamarpukur, where he was offered a house and an acre of good land to cultivate. Far from the bustle of cities, Ramakrishna's parents led a quiet family life in the simplicity of the countryside, its cadence set by the strict observance of their religious obligations and the ritual feasts.

Mahendra Nath Gupta recounts in his *Gospel* that Ramakrishna said of his mother:

that she was the personification of rectitude and kindness and everyone always loved her for the generosity of her heart. My father, whose probity was inviolable, never accepted gifts from the *sudras*. He spent much of his time in adoration and prayer, repeating the name of God and chanting the sacred hymns. When in his hours of meditation he invoked the goddess Gayatri, his chest grew flushed and his eyes were filled with tears. He devoted his leisure to weaving garlands for the Divine Family, Raghuvir. (Introduction to *The Gospel of M.*, page 3.)

Ten years after he had moved to Kamarpukur, Khudiram made a pilgrimage to Rameswar, at the southern tip of India. Two years later his wife gave birth to a second son, who was named Rameswar. Then, in 1835,

❊

43

Kamarpukur

The birthplace

when he was sixty years old, Khudiram made another pilgrimage, this time to Gaya, the holy place that is marked with the imprint of Vishnu's foot. There the god appeared to him during a dream and promised to be reincarnated in Khudiram's next son. Chandra Devi too had a vision in front of the temple of Shiva in Kamarpukur, a vision that foretold the birth of a divine child. On his return, Khudiram found her transfigured by the dazzling illumination that had thrown her into a swoon. She was pregnant. The child who was to grow into a prodigy from the spiritual point of view, and who is known now under the name of Ramakrishna, was born on February 18. In memory of the dream at Gaya, he was named Gadadhar, for this

❈

45

name, which means "the Bearer of the Scepter," is one
of the many others that belongs to Vishnu.

Intelligent, precocious, endowed with a remarkable
memory, sound of body and keen of mind, Gadadhar
grew bigger and quickly learned to read and write in
school. His father taught him the names of his ancestors, which he retained with the same facility with
which he memorized the hymns that he was to address
to the gods and goddesses. The child showed genuine
talents for sculpture, painting, and singing, but more
than anything he loved the epic tales of Hindu mythology. Only arithmetic inspired him with an aversion
that he could not conquer.

First Ecstasy

Young Gadadhar experienced his first ecstasy when
he was six years old.

One day in June or July, as he was walking along a narrow
path among the rice fields and eating puffed rice that he
was carrying in a basket, he looked up at the sky and
saw a beautiful dark storm cloud, which quickly spread
until it filled the entire sky. Above him passed a flight of
snow-white geese. The beauty of the contrast made him
lose consciousness, and he fell in a faint, his rice scatter-
ing about him. A passing peasant found him, picked
him up, and carried him to his parents' house. (Introduction to *The Gospel of M.*, page 4.)

Ramakrishna declared later that, having fallen into an ecstasy for the first time, he had experienced indescribable joy.

When Gadadhar was seven his father died. This loss, which was a great grief for him, taught him to understand the impermanence of beings and of things. While he devoted himself to assisting his mother in the accomplishment of her household tasks, the child also spent long periods absorbed in his own thoughts. He began to read more, especially the religious histories contained in the *Puranas,* which fascinated him quite as much as the tales told by pilgrims or monks making pilgrimages who stopped at Kamarpukur on their way to the shrine of Puri. He performed various services for them and watched them during their meditations.

Brahmin Initiation

At the age of nine little Gadadhar was presented with the sacred rope during the ceremony of initiation, or *Upanayana,* which celebrates the child's entrance into the Brahmin community—a privilege to which he was entitled because he was a Brahmin's son and that made him subject to certain disciplines. The caste of the Brahmins, the highest in India, is alone in its religious essence. It possesses spiritual authority, even though the other castes participate to varying degrees

❁

A Brahmin

in sacred matters. The Brahmins occupy the highest
rank in the Hindu social system. It is their duty to
teach the *Veda* and everything else that is in any way
sacerdotal in character. They serve as priests—in order
to be a priest one must be "born" a Brahmin by "sacri-
ficing" for others—and they are supported by the gifts
of the faithful.

Before it became the result of a state of affairs created
by birth, caste had been a compensation for one's occu-
pation. It was the duty of the fourth caste, that of the
sudras, to serve the first three castes—the Brahmins,
the *kshatriyas,* or warriors, and the *vaishyas,* or mer-

❋

chants—to the full extent of the servant capacities by performing manual labor, although certain forms of this work were reserved for the "untouchables," or *parias*.

Now on the day when Gadadhar received the sacred cord at his *Upanayana* he shocked his family. Disregarding the obligations of his caste, he accepted and ate a meal prepared by a *sudra* woman. At some earlier time he had promised this humble person that he would eat the food that she offered him. And he did not want to wound her feelings.

For the child who was still called Gadadhar the ceremony of initiation inaugurated a new life. He was permitted to worship Raghuvir (a name for Rama and the divine family of Ramakrishna) and to devote himself to meditation. He also dedicated himself to the adoration of the stone image (which was called *puia*), a rite both public and private.

Image worship is in fact quite widespread among the Hindus, although for the great majority of them the image is only a physical support for their adoration, an auxiliary of worship to the same extent as prayer or other outer religious practices.

As soon as Ramakrishna entered into contemplation, the Lord appeared to him virtually immediately. It was from this time forward that the propensity of his nature to lose consciousness became stronger.

While he was still very young he took part in a religious drama acted by a group of children of his own

❁

age; he played the part of Siva. He succeeded in identifying himself with the part to such a degree that he "streamed with tears of happiness." The supernatural gift that was never to leave him, the gift of "being able to embrace all the souls in the world," was already making itself evident in him. With his young friends he organized a small open-air theatrical company that enacted scenes selected from the stories of the heroes of the *Ramayana* and the *Mahabharata,* performing in the beautiful leafy shadows of the mango groves. His favorite themes dealt with Krishna's life in Vrindavan. Gadadhar was perfect in his impersonation of the youthful and somewhat feminine grace of Krishna, singing and dancing with that sense of music and rhythm that was inborn in him. In later years the slightest false note in the singing of his disciples would always make him smile.

Severe economic difficulties—Khudiram's widow endured some painful years—compelled Gadadhar's elder brother to go to Calcutta in order to open a Sanskrit school there. Ramkumar sent for Gadadhar, who was by then sixteen, to serve as his assistant in the school. For all his concentrated effort, Gadadhar proved unfit for this kind of work. He paid virtually no attention to the course of studies and invested all his enthusiasm in the illumination of religious images and the singing of the sacred hymns.

The image is only a material support for adoration. (Shown: Vishnu in the temple of Birla, Delhi)

When Ramkumar reproved him, Gadadhar replied that his sole wish was to acquire the wisdom that
would enlighten his heart and give him the complete
peace for which he yearned. He remembered the meditations of the monks whom he had served in his childhood. Their devotion, their purity of life, their abdica-
tion of the things of this world had left a permanent
mark on him. His only thought henceforth was to
emulate them.

His ideal was firmly fixed in God. Knowing that the
real stream of Indian life, the deepest life of this vast
people, is only spirituality, he wanted to continue the
way of his ancestors, the great sages who had represented the crests of the successive waves of that spirituality, through his own inner quest for the Divine. . . .
All the energies of his being were directed toward this
single goal: God and the knowledge of God.

In spite of the advice of Ramkumar, who would
have preferred to make his brother a brilliant student,
Gadadhar stood firm, and Ramkumar had to abandon
his ambitions. Another prospect was about to open
before Gadadhar and turn his destiny into quite a
different direction.

The Temple of Kali

At this time, *The Gospel of M.* tells us, there was a
rich widow living in Calcutta, Rani Rasmani, who was

The garden-temple of Dakshineswar on the bank of the Ganges

a member of the *sudra* caste. This woman was highly esteemed for her intelligence, her charitable works, and her devotion to God. Assisted in her endeavors by her brother-in-law, Mathur Babu, in 1847 Rani Rasmani commissioned the construction of a temple, not quite four miles from the Ganges, dedicated to her *ishta*, Kali, the Divine Mother.

This temple is still in existence. Here is Romain Rolland's description of it:

Ramakrishna's chamber, at the northwest corner of the courtyard immediately beyond the row of the twelve temples of Shiva, had a semi-circular veranda with a roof supported on columns, which overlooked the Ganges at the sunset. A tremendous hall for the presentation of music and sacred dramas opened on the large rectangular courtyard. Bedrooms for guests were laid out along the sides. There were kitchens for them and for the gods. A

beautiful tree-shaded garden stretched to the east and the north; it had two pools and it was meticulously cared for, rich in flowers and scents. Beyond it there is now a grove of five sacred trees, planted at the wish of Ramakrishna and made famous under the name of Panchavati. There he spent his days, meditating and speaking of the Divine Mother. Before him the Ganges murmured. (Rolland, *Life of Ramakrishna*.)

In the twelve small temples of Siva (or Shiva) the worshiper could contemplate the emblems of the great god of renunciation, the great Ascetic, adored daily according to specific rites. Offerings of white flowers, leaves of the *bel* tree, and a little water from the Ganges were sufficient to satisfy this great-hearted god and earn from him the reward of liberation.

Of the two temples situated in the center of the rectangular court, the smaller, facing the Ganges, is that of Radhakanta, or the temple of Vishnu, adorned with images of Radha and Krishna placed on a pedestal and symbolizing the union between the believer and God. The floor of the temple is paved in marble. Near the threshold was a font filled with holy water. Devoutly the faithful used to sip a few drops of it. The larger temple, facing the south, was dedicated to Kali, who was worshiped as *Bhavatarini,* or the Redeemer of the Universe. A basalt statue of the Divine Mother, clothed in gold brocade and wearing a crown and necklaces, as

The image of Kali in the temple of Dakshineswar

well as a garland of human heads, danced on the prostrate body of Siva, her husband.

One of her four hands held the sword and another offered her gifts. In the face of this representation of the Goddess, the faithful felt at the same time the terribleness of her destructive power and the assurance of her motherly tenderness. Is not Kali the incarnation of the cosmic power, the totality of the universe in the harmony between its opposing poles?

In the garden-temple of Dakshineswar the entire world was synthesized in a Trinity composed of Kali, Nature the Mother, of Siva, the Absolute, and of Radhakanta, Love. Kali was its pivot, its sovereign. It is she who creates, she who destroys, but she is greater and deeper still "for those who know how to see." She is the Universal Mother. Ramakrishna said:

My Holy Mother reveals herself to her children through the various forms of her Divine Incarnations. She is the visible God who leads the Elect to the invisible God, and, if it pleases her to do so, she strips every created being of the last trace of his ego in order to immerse him in the awareness of the Absolute, the undifferentiated God. Thanks to her, the finite ego, the *I,* is lost in the infinite Ego: *atman-Brahman.* (Rolland, *Life of Ramakrishna.*)

Rani Rasmani spent a fortune for the construction of the garden-temple of Dakshineswar and its appurtenances, and she spent another fortune for the ceremony of its dedication, which was held on May 31, 1855. Since she was a *sudra,* she found it difficult to enlist a

❈

Brahmin who would be willing to serve as a priest. After some hesitation on her part and a great deal of opposition on the part of his young brother Gadadhar, who at this time was still extremely rigid on the question of caste, Ramkumar finally gave way, and he was appointed to serve the temple of Kali.

A year later Ramkumar died and Ramakrishna decided to take his place. He too, however, evinced a certain hesitancy before he accepted. He had accompanied Ramkumar to Dakshineswar even though he thoroughly disapproved of his brother's having accepted the appointment. But the atmosphere of the temple and its surroundings, the holy solitude of the place, the respect shown to Ramkumar by Rani Rasmani and Mathur Babu, the proximity of the Ganges, that great sacred river, and above all the living presence of the Goddess, Kali, in the end overcame his last scruples.

Very rapidly Ramakrishna's religious zeal attracted the attention of Mathur Babu, who one day asked him to take part in the service of adoration in the temple of Kali. At about the same time, Ramakrishna's sixteen-year-old nephew, Hriday, an intelligent, industrious youth, arrived at Dakshineswar in search of employment. This visit, which gave Ramakrishna so much pleasure, induced him to become the officiant of the temple on condition that Hriday be made his assistant.

FOLLOWING PAGES A priestess of the temple of Kali on the bank of a branch of the Ganges at Calcutta

The nephew was later to play an important part in the uncle's life. Always quick to help him regardless of the cost in personal sacrifice, Hriday was to follow Ramakrishna everywhere, like his shadow, faithfully watching over him, especially during Ramakrishna's spiritual experiments, which were sometimes dangerous when they were of long duration.

The Priest of Kali

A major stage in Ramakrishna's life was beginning for him at Dakshineswar. He was twenty years old. He was a priest.

Having been born into an orthodox Brahmin family, he knew the temple liturgy, the various religious rituals that he had to fulfill in the course of the daily ceremonies. He knew above all that the innumerable gods of Hinduism represented only limited manifestations of the Spirit—the Infinite, not to be grasped by the finite intelligence of man.

But these divine, symbolic manifestations, which corresponded to human affinities, help those persons who know how to invoke them with fervor, how to gain the release from the world of phenomena and the ordeals that it entails in accord with each man's *karma*. The gods are only the intermediaries of the Source of all Light, of all Wisdom, of all Intelligence, which is the One without a second.

❀

As long as a man remains caught in the bonds of his personality, of his earthly desires, he can worship God only by those means that are accessible to him. Thus the *Sanatana-Dharma* calls on the believer to pray to God as an ideal Father, an ideal Mother, an ideal Friend, before adoring Him in spirit. For the Name, when spoken, leads to the Nameless, the Form to the Formless, the Word to Silence, Ecstasy to the serene Realization of Peace in the Absolute: *Satchitananda.* Gradually the gods are fused into a single deity. Until this culmination has been reached, the worshiper cannot dissociate human factors from his worship. And for worship he makes use of concrete objects, statues decked with vestments and jewels.

In the rites of adoration the Hindu priest, in whose body the various spiritual centers are aroused, invokes the Supreme Spirit in his heart in order that it may be transposed to the image that is before him. He no longer sees the clay or the stone in the image, but solely the surface of the Spirit, palpitating with life. After the act of adoration, the Supreme Spirit returns to its true sanctuary, the heart of the priest.

The pure believer recognizes the absurdity of worshiping transcendental Reality in a tangible image that is clothed or put to sleep according to the appropriate ritual when that transcendental Reality is incorporeal, cannot be limited by space and matter, penetrates the whole universe, and surpasses understanding. . . . But through these rites the true believer aspires to pass beyond words and praises, beyond the holiest of chants, to discover God as pure Awareness, in which he immerses himself and fuses himself, for it is only in God that he has life.

In actuality Ramakrishna was very quickly able to select the puissant Goddess whom he wished to serve. He allowed himself to be won little by little, then to be wholly captivated by the atmosphere of the temple of Kali. The Divine Mother seemed present to him. Soon she enveloped him. Whereas to the ignorant she represented only the Goddess of destruction, Ramakrishna found in her the unrivaled sweetness of maternal love. In his eyes she became the true synthesis of antinomies, the ultimate Divine in feminine form. She was the incarnation of the only Reality; henceforth the world was no more to him than an impalpable shadow. . . . His entire soul was engulfed in adoration of the Goddess, Kali.

What might be regarded by some as a derangement of the mind or a religious aberration confronts us, on the contrary, with an unprecedented spiritual manifestation; for, by way of this seeming mystical madness, Ramakrishna was to travel the various religious roads that some believers, even though privileged, devote their entire lives to learning.

Once he had undergone the special rite of initiation required of those who would be the priests of Kali, a strange transformation took place in Ramakrishna's spirit. When his *guru,* a qualified Brahmin, whispered

❀

Kali (Durga): she who creates, she who destroys

the sacred word into the ear of his *chela,* Ramakrishna felt a powerful shock and, uttering a loud cry, plunged into a profound concentration, which was to be the prelude to many more. . . . As the young priest pursued the performance of his duties, repeating the *mantras* as the Scriptures prescribed, he quickly grasped the secret meaning of the religious ritual.

❁

63

Ramakrishna's burning zeal increased unceasingly. Soon it knew no limitations. It was a delirium. Not only did he fulfill the obligations of his post as a priest with passion; he spent his hours of leisure in long meditations consecrated to Kali, his Divine Mother. He took over a wild, solitary place north of the temples, a kind of jungle of thick, thorny brush. There he spent whole nights in prayer. As he prayed he would remove his clothing, even the sacred cord that must never be taken off. One day he tried to explain his strange behavior to Hriday: "Do you not believe that, when one is thinking of God, one ought to free oneself of all one's bonds?" His nephew was disturbed and began to think that his uncle was losing his mind. (Introduction by Swami Nikhilananda to *The Gospel of M.*)

Visions

As his love for the Divine Mother grew deeper, Ramakrishna began to forget or to cut short, by reason of his excess of concentration, certain of the ritual passages of worship. Seating himself before the holy image, he no longer remembered to sing his hymn of joy to the Great Goddess. An overwhelming desire to see Kali filled his heart. He implored her. He begged her,

Another aspect of Kali: the symbol of the forces of nature, the synthesis of antinomies

❋

like a child who cries to its mother. Sometimes, in desperation, he beat his head against the floor and wept so bitterly that people thought that he had lost his own mother. In other moments, moments of doubt, he inveighed against Kali: "Do you exist, Mother, or are you a fiction of my mind, a poetic vision without any reality? Why can I not see you?" (Introduction to *The Gospel of M.*, page 13.)

Ramakrishna could neither eat nor sleep. Most of the time unaware of what went on about him, he behaved in a strange fashion that frightened his associates.

The sole purpose of his existence was to see the Divine Mother. The vision for which he had so consuming a desire was not to be withheld much longer; according to Swami Nikhilananda, Ramakrishna gave this description of it:

'One day I was torn by a terrible anguish. I felt that my heart was being wrung out like a wet cloth. Suffering was destroying me. At the thought that I might not have this divine vision, life no longer seemed to me to be worth living. Suddenly I saw the great sword that was hanging in the shrine. I decided to make an end of it. I threw myself forward like a demented man to seize it, and suddenly at last the Blessed Mother showed herself. The buildings in their various sections, the temple, and all the rest vanished before my eyes and left no trace. In their place I saw an ocean of consciousness without limits, infinite and splendid. As far as my eyes could see, I perceived brilliant waves that rose from all sides and broke over me with a terrifying roar, ready to drown me. I could no longer breathe. Caught in the whirlpool of

The Panchavati, a grove of trees beneath
which Ramakrishna withdrew to meditate

the waves, I fell lifeless. What was going on in the outer
world I had no idea. But within me a steady flow of indescribable felicity like nothing ever known pervaded my
whole being and I felt the presence of the Divine
Mother.' When he regained consciousness there was only
one word on his lips: 'Mother.' (Introduction to *The
Gospel of M.*, page 14.)

In discussing this vision, Ramakrishna's disciples
wondered whether he had actually seen the Divine
Form, but he did not say so. It was still only a foretaste
of the experiences that were going to follow, increasingly more lofty, increasingly more inexpressible.

From this time forward the priest of Kali desired
only the reappearance of that "flash" that had come
from the Mother, who had illuminated his sky. He
could no longer live without it. Ardently he yearned to
see her with his eyes open during his meditations. His
impatience became extreme. A terrible contest began.
Sometimes the Great Goddess appeared to him, some-

❋

The shrine of Kali at Dakshineswar

times his supplications were unanswered. Ramakrishna sobbed, his nerves were taut, his body shook with the force of his emotions. Suddenly he saw Kali, smiling, consoling him, instructing him. His happiness was beyond measure. During this period, in the intensity of his joys and his agonies, he experienced very rare spiritual states. But the shock that he had felt at the Divine Mother's first apparition had been so strong that at times he was no longer in control of himself. He lived through moments of real terror, in dread for his own sanity.

He prayed to Kali to come to his assistance. Now that he felt that the Great Goddess owned him totally, he abandoned his will to her. The "flash" that he had glimpsed on the first occasion materialized little by little into a physical shape, radiant as it emerged from an ocean of transparent mist with luminous waves of molten silver that surrounded it. In this hazy mist one day he saw first the Mother's feet, then her waist, then her upper body, her head, and finally all of her.

Insatiable, he was insanely eager to hear her breathe and speak. Often when he was engaged in adoration in the temple he went from immeasurable exaltation to the inertia of a stone, or he collapsed under the burden of his extreme emotion. Suddenly he began to dance, to sing, lapsing into childlike gambols before the statue of the Goddess. He went at times to the point of committing acts that were contrary to the religious tradition. As he offered a flower to the Goddess, he touched his

❀

own head or body or feet, and this constituted a sacrilegious gesture.

Later, almost two years before his death, he was to talk to Dr. Sarkar, who was treating him, about this incident of the flower, which, instead of offering it to Kali during the service of adoration, his hand had placed for a second on his own head. He added that a young acolyte had not dared to approach him and indeed had confided to him later: "I see a light in your face but I am afraid to go near you." (*The Gospel of M.,* page 891.)

Obsessed by his desire for Kali's presence, Ramakrishna stood endless vigil for her appearance. At night, when the rituals of the day had been completed, he could not sleep.

> From his own room he thought that he heard her climbing the stairs to the floor above with the light step of a happy girl, making the bracelets on her ankles ring. He thought that he saw her with her hair flowing over her shoulders and her dark silhouette standing out against the night sky as she looked out over the Ganges or toward the distant lights of Calcutta. (Introduction to *The Gospel of M.,* page 13.)

His people in the temple, believing that he must be ill, urged him to go and consult a well-known physician, but no remedy could heal him.

It was a fearful period. Ramakrishna had ventured on to perilous ground where his only guide was the Divine Mother herself. Unremittingly he prayed to her to sustain him, to explain to him the mystery that so anguished him.

I do not understand what is happening. I do not know the *mantras* and the Scriptures. Teach me, Mother, to find you. You alone can help me. Are you not my only refuge, my only guide? (Introduction to *The Gospel of M.*, page 15.)

The life-giving presence of the Divine Mother was never lacking to him in his distress and his doubts. To most people the behavior of the priest of Dakshineswar had become a scandal. But a reflection of his inner joy illuminated his face and impressed his intimates, even those who criticized him. They admitted, they recognized the purity, the sincerity, the integrity, the sanctity of Ramakrishna. Influenced by the great loftiness of spirit that they sensed, in the end they too saw when they were in his presence what the priest of Kali saw. This was how one day Mathur Babu, to whom the temple belonged, saw the Divine Mother in his friend's room.

Mathur Babu, moreover, profoundly stirred by the young priest's extreme zeal, could not help feeling a genuine respect when he entered the sanctuary at the hour of worship and, himself unnoticed, observed Ramakrishna. He, like Rani Rasmani, always defended Ramakrishna with exemplary loyalty against the general anger. As for Hriday, he was the filial guardian of the "madman of God" and attended to his most urgent needs. Without him his uncle would have died.

Ramakrishna's visions became more intense and more profound. He regarded himself as Kali's child, and on her he concentrated his spiritual life—in a word, all his life—beseeching her to make him do her will at every moment. He was her instrument. He no longer closed his eyes. Infinitesimal drops of blood appeared on his skin, his whole body was on fire. Intoxicated with divine love, he sang.

> Who is he who will ever be able to understand what Kali is? Even the six *darçanas* do not have the power to reveal it. (*The Gospel of M.,* page 106.)

One day Ramakrishna took a bit of the food intended for the Goddess and gave it to a starving cat. The temple custodian, outraged, went to complain to Mathur Babu. The priest of Dakshineswar described the incident thus:

> The Goddess disclosed to me in the temple of Kali that she had become everything. She showed me that each thing is filled with Consciousness. The statue is filled with Consciousness, the cups of water are Consciousness, the altar is Consciousness, the threshold is Consciousness, the marble floor is Consciousness, everything is Consciousness. Within the room each object was bathed in divine felicity. Opposite the temple of Kali I saw a wicked man, but in him too I saw the vibration of the power of the Divine Mother. That was why I fed that cat with the food that should have been offered to the Divine Mother. I clearly saw that everything, even the cat, was the Divine Mother. (Introduction to *The Gospel of M.,* page 16.)

Hanuman, the king of the monkeys, the symbol of
spontaneity and friendship (a modern representation)

At about the same period the young priest began to worship God in the attitude of *Bhakti*—that is, the servant in relation to his master. Seeking to emulate Hanuman, the god of the monkeys and disciple of Rama, who is the deification of the ideal servitor, Sri Ramakrishna, thanks to his marvelous gift for "becoming others," identified himself with Hanuman. He began to feel a tremendous love for Rama, thus incarnating the essence of the devotion that a servant feels toward his master. But, since he always carried his efforts at identification to extremes, he began to live on fruit and roots, and his movements began to resemble those of a monkey. His two protectors were soon frightened by this new attitude, but a miraculous vision of Sita, which was a great blessing for Ramakrishna, released him completely from his experiment as Hanuman.

This period, which was so important in Ramakrishna's life and in which many others would have lost their sanity, was a terrible ordeal for him. He himself, appraising long afterward the abyss that he had skirted, wondered how he had escaped it. He emerged, however, prepared to face new spiritual experiences that would amaze those who were to be the witnesses of them and those who, still later, would hear their eternally prolonged echo.

To those who might be astonished at the strange tendencies evidenced in Ramakrishna's life in the form of external actions that seem extravagant, inexplicable, characteristic almost of loss of reason in a man who was to attain to so lofty a spirituality, to become a kind of superman, one might reply that they were perhaps necessary in order to hasten his complete conquest of the Divine. Is it not through violence that one wins the kingdom of God? Let us recall the life of St. Francis of Assisi, which has some points in common with that of the priest of Kali. Both men were equally consumed by the same devouring inner flame that is the love of God.

In Ramakrishna everything was in motion at the same time. Into the furnace of his passion he cast his mind, his soul, his body. The gift was made without reservations. It is this that marks the greatness of the saint, the divine stamp. This he did, and the unflawed diamond came out of the matrix in unprecedented splendor. It was an agonizing period of life for one so young, a grievous period made more painful by hours of doubt, an exhausting period. How could the chance aberrations of a moral tornado count for anything in the face of such results?

Ramakrishna endured these ordeals with complete humility. His childlike innocence—the innocence of the Divine Mother's child—disarmed even those who could not understand him, who observed critically every strange detail of his behavior . . . instead of contemplating the splendid spiritual flowering of a soul.

But it is possible, too, to understand the stupefaction of his familiars and their rather sharp reactions to the sometimes disconcerting actions of the priest of Kali. Certain incidents alarmed Rani Rasmani and Mathur Babu in spite of their faith in their priest's sincerity. One in particular frightened them. The servitor of the temple was meditating one day at the hour of worship. Not far from him Rani Rasmani was praying distractedly. Ramakrishna read the profane thoughts that were occupying her, and he slapped her publicly. Everyone was outraged. Rani Rasmani herself remained calm, and nobly she deemed that she had been punished by the Divine Mother as she deserved.

The young priest's passionate love of God and his exceptional purity deeply impressed Rani Rasmani in his favor. In his biography of the saint of Dakshineswar, Swami Nikhilananda tells us that Rani Rasmani and her brother-in-law, having observed Ramakrishna's unhealthy nervous tension, conceived the notion of having him meet two young women with the thought that a more normal life would put an end to his strange conduct. But, the moment the two young women crossed the threshold of the room, Ramakrishna saw in them—as he was never to stop seeing in every woman as long as he lived—the manifestation of the Mother of the Universe, and he fell into an ecstasy as he murmured her name. In spite of this unshakable purity, which Rani Rasmani admired, she and Mathur Babu agreed that the celebrant of their temple ought to go for a while to visit his mother. Kept informed of the events that were occurring at Dakshineswar and eager

❈

to heal her son of what she called his divine madness, his mother asked him to come to see her. It was her intention to find him a bride. So Ramakrishna went to Kamarpukur.

The woman whom Ramakrishna was to marry in 1859, little Sarada Devi—who was five years old when he was twenty-three—lived in a village at Jayrambati, some two or three miles from Kamarpukur. In spite of her extremely tender age, she prayed to God to keep her from all taint, to allow her to remain always as pure and perfumed as a white flower. Looking at the full moon, she would cry out: "O God, there are spots even on the moon. Grant that I may have none." (*The Gospel of M.*, page 17.)

Hence she was fitting to be betrothed to the future saint of Dakshineswar. This was a union of souls, a marriage that was never to be consummated. Once the ceremony had been performed, little Sarada, as custom decreed, returned to her parents. A most special marital destiny was to be hers later, a destiny of abnegation, of silence, of constant self-effacement, indeed worthy of the bridegroom chosen for her, who was to lead her into the highest of spiritual paths.

Spiritual Experiences

Ramakrishna remained in Kamarpukur for a little more than a year after the celebration of his wedding.

❋

Then, his health having been completely restored, he went back to Dakshineswar. But he had barely entered the temple of Kali when he was caught up again, and more violently than ever, in his religious delirium. *The Gospel of M.* portrays him plunging himself into the same meditations followed by ecstasies, experiencing again the same feeling that his body was on fire, the same fits of sobbing, the same indifference to the outer world. His visions increased and became fearful. All that he desired now was to subject himself to harsh disciplines in order to rid himself of every obstacle to his spiritual advancement. First he purged himself of any desire for gold and women (*kamini kanchana*). No doubt this imposed no great effort on him, since he had never felt the slightest ardor in the presence of women, having always regarded every woman only as a manifestation of the Divine Mother; but it was important to him to offer a symbolic proof. One day he took a rupee in one hand and a bit of earth in the other, then threw both into the Ganges with contempt. He sought also to extirpate from his mind the idea of the inequality of castes, and he went to visit a *paria* in order to clean his house with his long hair, which he had neglected for far too long. "Those who love God belong to no caste," he declared. (*The Gospel of M.*, page 154.)

For months he was completely without sleep. A *sannyasin* whom he had met before appeared to him again and ordered him to concentrate even more on God. He implored the Mother. She sustained him for the next two years in the alternations of his passion and his desperation.

In 1861 Rani Rasmani went from this world into the other, and, after her death, her brother-in-law, Mathur Babu, became the sole owner of the temple. He placed his person and his fortune at Ramakrishna's disposition. As soon as the priest of Kali voiced a wish, Mathur fulfilled it. For Ramakrishna (who acknowledged the fact with gratitude) he was one of the five benefactors chosen by the Divine Mother to watch over her "child" and take care of his material existence.

It was at this time that a providential meeting was to put an end to his mystic madness and open as yet unsuspected prospects to him.

Tantrism

One day a Brahmin woman who was to play a major part in Ramakrishna's spiritual development appeared at Dakshineswar. Born in Bengal, she was an adept of the Tantric and Vaishnavite modes of worship. Some fifty years old, still beautiful, clad in the orange robe of a *sannyasin,* she brought as her only belongings two garments and a few books.

As soon as she saw the priest of Kali, who welcomed her with much deference, the woman, who was always known as the *Bhairavi Brahmani,* the Brahmin nun, began to weep. "My son," she said, "you are he after whom I have so long searched." Ramakrishna described for her the experiences and the visions that most people regarded as symptoms of lunacy. She replied: "My son, in this world everyone is mad. Some are mad for money, some are mad for creatures, some are mad for luxury or fame. You are mad for God." (Introduction to *The Gospel of M.,* page 18.)

The Brahmin woman reassured Ramakrishna. She taught him that he had passed through the highest states of *sadhana* (spiritual discipline), states that are in general almost unknown and that are described in the *Bhakti* Scriptures; he had even attained to *mahabhava,* the supreme rapture that crowns all others. She told him too to rejoice that he had been able to scale each step in the bitter ascent by his own strength, without a guide. None of his sufferings had been in vain. Each ranked among those set forth in the texts. Theretofore the Scriptures had recorded only the experiences of Sri Radha and Sri Chaitanya as having known this sublime state of exaltation.

A parent-son relationship was soon established between the Brahmin nun and the priest of Kali. He looked on her as his mother and she regarded him as the child, Krishna.

But, in order to make him fully aware of the road of

Ramakrishna in *samadhi* during a *kirtan* in the house of Keshub. He is supported by Hriday

Illumination that he had traveled alone and blindly, at the cost of painful ordeals, the *Bhairavi* helped him with her enlightenment to travel once more the various paths of *sadhana* and to take the nineteen positions before the Divine. Together, then, they repeated the same experiences. Day after day she kept watch over his ecstasies during the *kirtan,* the meditation, and the *samadhi.* Recognizing his remarkable power of transmitting his own spiritual vigor to others, she arrived at the conclusion that such results could be obtained only by a highly developed soul. Only a Divine Incarnation was capable of such manifestations. She redoubled her attention and her care, and she revealed to her *chela* the paths that she herself had taken, instructing him in the method that the Holy Books ordain for avoiding the dangers along the way. And she openly proclaimed that Ramakrishna, like Sri Chaitanya, was an Incarnation God. (Sri Chaitanya, born in Bengal in 1485 and regarded as a Divine Incarnation, had been a great Vishnuite prophet. He had asserted that singing the name of God without rest was the most efficacious of prayers, the best discipline for the epoch of Kaliyuga, which is our own.)

When the young priest told Mathur what the Brahmin woman had said to him, Mathur shook his head. He hesitated to believe that his priest was an *Avatar* comparable to Rama, Krishna, or Chaitanya, even though he acknowledged the extraordinary spirituality of the officiant of his temple. Nevertheless he bowed to the Brahmin's request and organized a meeting of theologians for the purpose of discussing the case of Ramakrishna. This conference was held in the *nat-mandir* (music auditorium) opposite the temple of Kali.

The two most famous *pandits* of the time were invited: Vaishnavcharan and Gauri, both escorted by professors and adepts. While the Brahmin nun put forward her observations with emphasis on certain especially important points of theology and with such knowledge of the Scriptures and such competence that she was able to answer all the *pandits'* questions, Ramakrishna, seated like a child in the center of their circle and indifferent to what was going on around him, was wholly lost in his own thoughts. Sometimes smiling, sometimes chewing on a little pinch of spices, he turned toward Vaishnavcharan with a spark of malice in his eyes as if to say: "See, this too is how I am." This little scene in the bosom of this learned assemblage was revealing of the highly complex nature of this singular being who unceasingly skirted the plane of the Absolute while remaining on that of *Maya,* which is the everyday.

At the end of the meeting, Vaishnavcharan proclaimed his full agreement with the Brahmin nun, acknowledging that Ramakrishna had attained to *mahabhava,* the sure indication of the extremely rare manifestation of the Divine in a man. When the other persons in attendance, particularly those attached to the service of the garden temple, heard this announcement, they were struck dumb. Looking at Mathur, Rama-

❈

krishna cried out like a child: "What a surprise! He too says that. I'm glad to learn that I'm not ill after all." (Introduction to *The Gospel of M.,* page 19.)

Pandit Gauri shared the view of his colleague and of the Brahmin nun. In fact, when Ramakrishna repeated to him what Vaishnavcharan had said, Gauri replied: "Is that really all that he said about you? It is not very much, at bottom. I am fully convinced that you are part of that source of spirituality of which a small part descends to earth from time to time in the form of an Incarnation." And, when Ramakrishna said with a smile that Gauri was "overdoing it" in comparison to Vaishnavcharan, the young priest added: "What then have you seen in me that allows you to form such an opinion?"

Gauri responded: "My heart knows it by intuition and the Scriptures confirm it to me. I am prepared to prove what I am saying to anyone who may challenge me." The worshiper of Kali thereupon concluded: "Good, it is you who say this, but, believe me, I know nothing of all this." (Introduction to *The Gospel of M.,* page 20.)

Thus it was the most eminent theologians of his time who proclaimed that the priest of Dakshineswar, treated by his associates as a sick man, was really in their view a Divine Incarnation.

Once such a judgment had been handed down, Ramakrishna was still what he had always been, the simplest of men, content to point out that this pronouncement could make no change in his spirit. In fact it displeased him when people spoke of his *Avatar*. Hoping to remain a scholar all his life, he often repeated an axiom to his disciples: "The longer I live, the more I learn." (Introduction to *The Gospel of M.*, page 20.)

In his Introduction to *The Gospel,* on which we have so largely drawn, Swami Nikhilananda also says that, under the Brahmin nun's guidance, the young priest began to practice the various disciplines embraced in the sixty-four principal books of the *Tantras*. According to this doctrine, the Ultimate Reality is *chit,* or Awareness, which is identical with *sat,* or Being, and *ananda,* or Bliss. *Satchitananda* represents the Absolute, or Reality, preached in the *Vedas*. And man is identical with this Reality. But, under the influence of *Maya,* he has forgotten his true nature and he believes the *unreal* world, the merely apparent world round him, to be *real*. This error engenders his own limitations and sufferings, for the goal of the spiritual disciplines is precisely that of making man rediscover his identity with the Real.

Whereas the *Vedanta* proposes, in order to obtain this result, an austere and arduous method that can be pursued only by those exceptionally endowed with intelligence and will power, Tantrism is inclined to a greater indulgence and takes human weakness into consideration. It combines philosophy and religious ritual, meditation and ceremonial, renunciation and the joy of living. Hoping thus to lead the student

85

gradually toward his supreme identification with the Divine through the sublimation of his desires and his pleasures, this philosophy does not imply the abrupt renunciation of the outer world, for that world with all its manifestations is only the "game" (*lila*) of Siva and his *sakti,* Kali, of the Absolute and its *impenetrable* Power.

But the Tantric rites are extremely dangerous to follow without the help of a highly qualified *guru* who can prevent his *chela* from losing his balance. In Tantrism, Siva, who represents the Absolute, is a more or less passive principle, whereas Kali, on the contrary, incarnates the great active force of the universe as well as the Divine Mother of whom all women are symbols. The meditation on Kali that was Ramakrishna's unceasing practice constitutes the central discipline of the *Tantras.*

Ramakrishna required barely three days to reach the designated goal of each of the Tantric works. Once he had carried out the preliminary rites, he was seized with a Divine Fervor that carried him to *samadhi.* Evil ceased to exist for him. The word *flesh* lost all meaning. His life in the world consisted only of the game of Siva and his *sakti.* Everywhere he contemplated the power and the manifest beauty of the Divine Mother. *Everything* was pervaded with Awareness and Felicity. Then he had a vision of the Ultimate Cause of the universe in the form of an immense glowing triangle giving birth every second to an infinite number of

❀

Kali showing the *sakra*, the wheel that is the symbol of the nervous center through which the *Kundalini* runs in order to accomplish the unity of consciousness worlds. He heard the *Anahata Sabda,* the great sound, *Aum,* of which all the uncountable sounds in the universe are only echoes. Thus he gained the eight supernatural powers of *Yoga,* which make a man almost omnipotent, but immediately he cast them aside with disdain as being of no worth to the spirit. In his vision he perceived the Divine *Maya* by whom the universe is created and sustained and in whom it is finally absorbed.

It was at this stage in the life of the priest of Kali that the *Kundalini Sakti* was awakened in him; rising from the base of the spinal column, it rose through the six centers of the mystic canal of the *Sushumna* to the top of his head, the *Sahasrara,* the thousand-petaled lotus. The awakening of the *Kundalini* is the beginning of spiritual consciousness and of union with Siva in the *Sahasrara,* which culminates in *samadhi.*

It is here that the Tantric disciplines come to an end.

Vishnuism

Guided by his *guru,* the Brahmin nun, Ramakrishna thereupon embarked on the disciplines of Vishnuism, the sect of the worshipers of Vishnu, who is also adored under the names of Hari and Narayana. Of the many incarnations of Vishnu the most illustrious are those of Rama and Krishna. Vishnuism is in the highest sense the religion of *Bhakti,* of love. Here it is not logic or metaphysics that leads to the Divine; it is, rather, a passionate attachment to the Lord.

The *bhakta* must begin with dedication to an aspect of God, or *ishta,* that he has chosen. As a result of successive states of adoration, he succeeds in attaining to his ideal, seeing it, and conversing with it. Thereafter the presence of his Lord becomes living and almost permanent because concentration is sufficient to make his *ishta* appear. For the priest of Kali the vision of his *ishta,* the Divine Mother, filled his life; she had become all forms and penetrated all forms. He had reached the hyperconscious spiritual state in which all of what is material vanishes and only the Divine remains. This is union with *Brahman.*

Even if heavenly happiness were offered to the *bhakta,* he would refuse it, because his one desire is to love beyond all limitations, in pleasure and in pain, in life and in death, in honor and in dishonor, in prosperity and in adversity. *Bhakti* is love without limit. Now the heart of Ramakrishna was made for the infinity of love.

In order to develop this love of God better in the believer's heart, Vishnuism humanizes God, who can be regarded and loved as a parent, a master, a friend; but, in direct proportion to this ascent in adoration, the personifications are erased and the believer discovers true communion with God himself. Then nothing more keeps him apart from his ideal; no social or

FOLLOWING PAGES Temple of Vishnu regarded as a sun god (driving the chariot of the sun) at Hampi

❦

moral obligation can bind to earth the spirit that has made its leap toward the Divine. In this the Vishnuite differs from the Vedantist, who endeavors to transcend all the varities of relations between subject and object, whereas the Vishnuite seeks only to remain in the love of God with his own personality. For him God is not the intangible Absolute but the Supreme Person.

An admirable illustration of Vishnuite adoration is that in the episode of Vrindavan in the *Bhagavata,* in which the shepherdesses love the shepherd, Krishna. He is their beloved. They surround him with their presences and their spirits and their souls. It is total love. Radha is the favorite among the shepherdesses because, since her love is the most ardent, she is the closest to Krishna. She has succeeded in achieving *mahabhava* and has been joined with her beloved. By means of language understandable through the senses this union represents an experience beyond the senses.

. . . By now people were coming from everywhere to see Ramakrishna. His reputation was established. Pilgrims crowded to the temple, knowing that the Master had succeeded in reaching God along many of the roads that lead to him.

Romain Rolland wrote in this connection:

Monks, scholars, ascetics, illuminated *sadhus* came to ask him for counsel and to be inspired by him who, seated now at the crossroads, dominated them. Their accounts

Vishnu: in three leaps he can measure the earth

tell of the fascination that was created by the appearance of him who returned—not, like Dante, from hell, but from the deep sea, like a pearl-fisher—of the golden radiance of his body, long tempered and given a patina by the fire of ecstasy. (This effect of great ecstasy, caused by the rush of blood, is constantly noted in India according to the observations of the Yogis; and later it will be seen that Ramakrishna, when he visits a religious man, makes certain with his first look at his host's chest that he has indeed passed through the fire of God. (Romain Rolland, *Life of Ramakrishna,* page 63.)

The *Vedanta*

Proud of her one *chela,* the Brahmin nun had followed his progress at first with astonishment and then with enthusiasm and admiration. For three years she had taught him everything that she knew, but the Divine Mother had not allowed her son to rest: Ramakrishna had to go beyond the visions and the ecstatic dreams of dualism. A new experience was awaiting him. The Brahmin nun felt that he needed a new mentor, that her child was growing away from her. The *guru* who was to take her place, an austere wandering monk, possessed a higher spiritual power and he was to introduce his influence at the precise time when the young priest, after his devotion to a personal

Krishna: with his music he enchants all creatures

❀

God, was about to learn the practice of devotion to the impersonal God.

Totapuri, "the naked man," as Ramakrishna familiarly called him because of his renunciation of all subjects and objects of earthly attachment, brought a philosophy that he had tested over forty years and that had made him a great ascetic. This Hindu philosophical system—the *Vedanta,* one of the six orthodox *darçanas*—is nondualist, *Brahman* being its sole reality. In it there is no time, no space, no causality, no multiplicity, all of these being mere appearances created by *Maya.*

The discipline of the *Vedanta* is one of negation: *neti.* Everything that is unreal is altogether denied and rejected in order to allow the emergence of the Unique Spirit, eternal and immutable and without parallel. This is the road of Knowledge, or *Jnana,* the direct road of the Absolute, *advaita* or nondualism, which is summarized in that maxim of the *Upanishads, tat tvam asi*—"You yourself are It." This great *mantra,* put forward by Sankara about 800 B.C., forms the credo of *advaita* or nondualism. Only the ONE exists. If we live in God, what is manifest disappears; if we live in the world, God no longer exists.

It was at the end of 1864 that Totapuri arrived at the garden-temple of Dakshineswar. Born probably in the Punjab, he headed a monastery in that part of India and proclaimed himself the leader of seven hundred *sannyasins.* Trained from his earliest youth in the methods of the *Advaita-Vedanta,* he looked on the

❁

world as a mere illusion. The numerous gods and goddesses of the dualist system, in his view, were mere fantasies of overtaxed minds. Completely indifferent to ceremonies, ritual, prayers, and the tangible objects of the phenomenal world, he had finally achieved his identity with the Absolute.

Wandering about the world like a soul set free of its chains, and unquestionably led by the Divine Will, he halted at Dakshineswar and very soon discovered that Ramakrishna was ready to become a student of the *Vedanta*. When the priest of Kali agreed, on condition that he obtain the Divine Mother's permission, Totapuri explained to him that in order to receive the teaching of the *Vedanta* he must become a simple monk. Ramakrishna assented to this, stipulating that the ceremony of his initiation should be performed in secret in order not to wound the feelings of his old mother, who was now living with him in the monastery.

Very early in the morning of the appointed day, a fire was lighted in the Panchavati and the two men, so different in appearance, seated themselves before it. Then Ramakrishna solemnly renounced all ties with his family, his friends, his own ego. The fire ritually consumed all his privileges in the form of emblems, among them his Brahmin's cord. After having stripped naked and conducted his own funeral service, the disciple received from his *guru* the ocher robe of the *sannyasin*—the symbol of his new Vedantic existence.

This was the beginning of the Master's teaching of

❀

his pupil—the teaching of the great truths of the *Vedanta. Brahman,* the Master said, is the sole Reality, always pure, always illumined, always free, beyond the limitations of time, space, and causes. It is within the power of *Maya* to fragment *Brahman* into Names and Forms. One must free oneself from this unreal prison and discover the true essence, that of one's identity with *Brahman,* in order to be fused with it in *samadhi.*

This is what the neophyte said after the initiation:

> The naked man (Totapuri) asked me to detach my mind from all objects and plunge deeply into *atman.* But, in spite of all my efforts, I could not cross the World of Name and Form and lead my mind to the "unconditioned" state. I had no difficulty in detaching my mind from all objects except the too familiar form of the radiant Mother, the essence of Pure Awareness, who appeared before me like a living Reality. Her magic smile barred my road to the beyond. I made a number of attempts to concentrate my spirit on the teachings of *advaita.* Each time the form of the Mother prevented me. I said to Totapuri: "It is impossible; I cannot elevate my spirit to the unconditioned state to place myself face to face with the *atman.* (Introduction to *The Gospel of M.,* page 29.)

"You must," Totapuri commanded sternly. "You should," he added. Then, looking round him and seeing a piece of glass, he picked it up and thrust its point between the eyebrows of his *chela,* crying: "Concentrate your mind on this point." Ramakrishna obeyed. He related afterward that, as soon as the Divine

Mother's form appeared to him again, he slashed the vision in two, using his thought as a sword. This last barrier having finally fallen, his spirit raised itself above the level of phenomena and he was lost in *nirvikalpa-samadhi.*

Thus he remained for three days, totally inert. Surprised by this unexpected outcome, Totapuri demanded: "Is it possible that he has gained in a single day what cost me forty years of effort?" (*The Gospel of M.,* page 29.)

This orthodox monk, the naked man, who never stayed more than three days in one place, remained at Dakshineswar for eleven months. He too had something to learn.

The physical constitutions of the two men made a contrast as striking as that between the oak and the reed. Totapuri, with his great height, was almost the archetype of male strength and resistance to any ordeal; whereas Ramakrishna, slender and frail and feminine in his sensitivity, gave an impression of weakness. Yet he was not at all weak. He had the endurance and the elasticity that make it possible to overcome any obstacle.

He had just provided dramatic proof of that by attaining to *nirvikalpa-samadhi,* the loftiest, the most difficult of all *samadhis,* in which subject and object vanish at the same time. Such an experience can be undergone only at the cost of a terrible shock that has a violent effect on the body and the mind of the believer

❊

who has plunged himself into it. Consciousness seems to have been annihilated, consumed in the excess of light that suffuses it. It is pointed out in the Books of the *Vedanta* that after this experience the body becomes like a withered leaf and dies. Only those who are born with special missions to be fulfilled on earth can come down again from such an altitude and resume normal lives. Invested with the supreme power, the Scriptures say, they remain in the world to help mankind. They are radiant with Divine Glory.

The priest of Kali had really lived the three ways of attaching oneself to Reality that are described by the *Vedanta*. The first attitude is illustrative of the dualist position and is expressed by the faithful in these words: "O Lord, when I am conscious of my body, my relation with you is that of the servant toward his master." The second is illustrative of the modified dualist position (*vishitadvaita*) and its verbalization is: "Lord, when I am conscious of being the *jiva*, I feel that I am part of you." The third, that of *advaita* or nondualism, is expressed thus: "When I am conscious of being *atman*, I am but one with you, I am you."

It was this third attitude that Ramakrishna had just learned in *nirvikalpa-samadhi,* the ultimate point of the *Vedanta* and the summit of his trials with Totapuri.

Even though he believed, with his *guru,* that the world is a mere illusory appearance, the saint of Dakshineswar accepted the power of *Maya* in the phenom-

❧

enal world. Full of respect and love, he looked on it as an aspect of *Brahman,* a mysterious and majestic expression of Divinity. To him *Maya* was God because everything is God. What he had just discovered on the transcendental plane he had found everywhere about him in the World of Names and Forms of that same *Maya,* a transparent veil that hides Reality from us, a veil woven by Kali, the Primordial Force, the Great Creator, who can no more be detached from *Brahman* than the power to burn can be separated from the fire. It is she who projects the world and causes it to vanish. Even those who attain to *nirvikalpa-samadhi* remain subject to her law as long as they remain on the relative plane.

Therefore, after his recent and far-reaching experience, Ramakrishna had a new vision of *Maya,* for her exclusive, dominant *rôle* had disappeared in his view. To him the world was now nothing but the glorious manifestation of the Divine Mother *become Brahman.* He understood that she called on him not to lose himself in the Absolute but to remain in the phenomenal world in order to help mankind. He obeyed. He spent the rest of his life divided between the two levels, now adoring the personal God, now worshiping the impersonal God, dedicated wholly to the Divine Mother even when he was serenely absorbed into the ocean without a shore that is the Absolute, between the immanent and the transcendent. Is this not a unique experience in the religious history of mankind? Or at

❀

least is it not an astounding example to which it is permitted to us to approach as a result of the wealth of testimony that surrounds the memory of this illuminated man?

The exchange with his *chela* was equally fruitful for Totapuri, who would no longer be the same when he left the garden-temple. A convinced and unshakable monist, he did not understand the worship of a personal God, Ramakrishna's love for Kali, or the significance of *Maya* and the relativity of the world. He believed only in the unreality of the phenomenal plane and accepted only the Absolute as it is taught in the *Vedanta*. He despised and ridiculed rites and prayers and songs and dances. But one day, *The Gospel* tells us when the *guru* and his disciple were talking of the *Vedanta,* a temple servant came to take a glowing coal from the sacred fire, which, as a symbol, was always burning, in order to light his cigarette, and he passed close to the great ascetic. Totapuri flew into a rage and almost struck the servitor. Sri Ramakrishna began to laugh, and he shouted: "What a disgrace! You have explained to me the reality of *Brahman* and the illusion of the world, and you all but hit a man in an access of impatience!" Embarrassed, Totapuri said nothing. He had experienced the power of *Maya*. (*The Gospel of M.,* page 31.)

Suddenly Totapuri was prevented from meditation by a violent attack of dysentery that caused him atrocious suffering. Unable to endure it longer and seeing the misery of this body that no longer obeyed him, he resolved—since a free soul does not admit domination by the flesh—to go and cast it into the Ganges. He walked into the river but he could not drown himself. A force greater than his own compelled him to return to the shore. Suddenly a dazzling light enveloped him and then on all sides he saw the presence of the Divine Mother.

> She was in each object, she was each object, she was in the water, she was the land, she was the body, she was the spirit, she was pain, she was knowledge, she was ignorance, she was life, she was death . . . she was everything that could be seen, heard, or imagined. She was the *Brahman* that Totapuri had worshiped all his life. (*The Gospel of M.,* page 31.)

Totapuri went back to Dakshineswar and spent the rest of the night in meditation on the Divine Mother. In the morning, accompanied by Ramakrishna, he went to the temple of Kali and prostrated himself before the statue of the Goddess. Then he realized that he had spent eleven months in Dakshineswar and, having bidden farewell to his *chela,* he resumed his life of wandering, but now he too had had illumination.

Later the priest of Kali summarized the meaning of the Vedantist ascetic's teaching:

> When I evoke the Supreme Being at rest, not creating, not preserving, not destroying, I call him *Brahman.* When I picture him to myself as active, creating, preserving, and destroying, I call him *Sakti* or *Maya,* or *Prakriti,* the

personal God. But the distinction thus made between these two aspects does not mean a difference. The personal God and the impersonal God are one and the same thing, like milk and its whiteness, the diamond and its brilliance. It is impossible to conceive the one without the other. The Divine Mother and *Brahman* are ONE. (*The Gospel of M.,* page 32.)

After his *guru*'s departure, Ramakrishna spent six months in a state of absolute identity with *Brahman,* a state from which as a rule no one returns and that can be prolonged hardly more than three weeks and never

The temple of Kali, between the small temples of Siva, at Dakshineswar

much more. "I was no longer aware of day and night," he said. "The flies could enter my mouth and my nostrils, as they enter those of a corpse, but I did not feel them. My hair was covered with dust." (*The Gospel of M.*, page 32.)

The priest of Kali would assuredly not have survived this extended experience without the attentive and constant devotion of a monk, a relative who had just arrived at Dakshineswar and who was to spend almost eight years with him. Mathur Babu had besought him to assume the duties of the officiant of the temple when the state of Ramakrishna's health had aroused such deep anxieties. Haladari had recognized that for the welfare of humanity he must stand guard over the person of "the madman of God." On a number of occasions he endeavored by violent means to bring back the soul to the prison of the body that it had deserted. He was able even to force a little food into the mouth of the man who, moreover, had been ordered by the Divine Mother to remain "on the threshold of relative consciousness." A short time later, Ramakrishna was stricken, like Totapuri, by a serious attack of dysentery. His body was tortured by pain, and this made it possible for his spirit gradually to return to the physical plane. Once he had been cured of his disease and had regained a state of calm and balance, he seemed to everyone to be a man who had returned to normality. His experiment was over, and he had emerged from it almost miraculously, he admitted later.

❈

Islam and Christianity

It is Asia that was the birthplace of the Prophets and the great spiritual Masters. It is Asia that was the theater of growth of the great religions. And of tolerance as well. Indeed, there are many illustrious representatives of tolerance in Asia. Among the innumerable examples of this tolerance so characteristic of the majority of Oriental religions there are those of Cyrus toward the Jews; and of the Tang emperors whose capital tolerated all sects, Nestorians, Manicheans, Jews; of the Mongols who invaded China, India, and Persia but did not persecute any of the established religions; of Emperor Akbar, who permitted the practice of the most diverse religions in his court. And did not Emperor Kang-Hi listen to the Jesuits in the seventeenth century?

These few instances of understanding and respect for the beliefs of others are still more numerous in our own time, but the most significant example, which seems to dominate all others, is that one that is so close to us, the example of Sri Ramakrishna, in this respect one of the most remarkable saints among all those who have been the light of the world.

As a result of the recent and decisive Vedantic experiments that had led him to *nirvikalpa-samadhi* under the guidance of his *guru,* Totapuri, the priest of the garden-temple could no longer endure the com-

❁

106

Indian Muslims at prayer at the Great Mosque of Delhi

pany of people who were still plunged in "the world of women and gold"—*kamini kanchana*—a Bengali locution that occurs so frequently in his utterances and that is quoted by his historian, who so faithfully transcribed all the sayings of the Master. The world of women and gold, in Ramakrishna's view, represented the major obstacle to anyone who wished to enter on the path of spirituality.

The sanctity of the temple and above all the sanctity of Ramakrishna himself drew a never-ending throng of pilgrims to Dakshineswar: monks, *sadhus* of every denomination, monists and dualists, Vaishnavites, Vedantists, and many more as well. The officiant of

❋

the temple welcomed them all with the same satisfaction which was all the keener because his greatest delight was in religious exchanges. Mathur was generous in his provision of food and clothing for the arriving pilgrims. Ramakrishna, though he knew nothing of books, possessed an amazing philosophical background that he had gained through his communication with ascetics and scholars.

It was his custom to say that, when the flowers open, the bees come of themselves to draw off the juice from which they make their honey. Now souls were flocking to Dakshineswar to assuage their hunger for God. He who yearned toward God had become a Master. Gauri, the great theologian who had been one of the first to announce that Sri Ramakrishna was indeed a Divine Incarnation, visited the priest of Kali in 1870 and, having received his benediction, renounced the world.

Narayan Shastri, another great *pandit,* who had studied the six *darçanas* of Hinduism, acknowledged that the adorer of the Divine Mother had gained in the ideal life what he himself had been able to learn only by reading the Holy Books. He too begged Ramakrishna to give him initiation. Soon Ramakrishna was surrounded by a circle of the "devout." They came from everywhere, and they were to continue doing so until his death.

After he had achieved *nirvikalpa-samadhi,* the young priest understood that the gods of the various religions were merely aspects of the Absolute, and that the Ultimate Reality could not be expressed in any human language. He felt that every religion led its believer to the same goal, *God*. Hence he grew impatient to try the paths of the other religions, having learned all the ways of his own.

One day he met a Muslim, Govinda Rai, and observed his devotion to his prayers. Ramakrishna saw that this man was truly illumined by the presence of God, that he too had found God. He asked the Muslim to grant him initiation. Thereupon he lived this new religious experience as he had the capacity to live each of them in all its fullness. For some time he continually repeated the name of Allah, he dressed as a Muslim, and he practiced the spiritual disciplines of Islam. He forgot the Hindu gods and goddesses, even Kali, and no longer visited their temples. After three days, a radiant countenance, that of Muhammad, appeared to him in a vision. Thus he came to know the Prophet of the Muslims. Then he entered into communion with *Brahman*. The powerful river of Islam had carried him back to the shoreless ocean of the Absolute. He had gone from the personal to the impersonal God. It was at the end of 1866 that this experience took place.

Eight years later, in November, 1874, Sri Ramakrishna heard the Bible being read in a garden at Dakshineswar and was seized with the desire to know Christianity. At once he dedicated himself to the task with zeal. Fascinated by the personality, the life, and the teaching of Jesus, he was sitting one day in the

❈

drawing room of Jadu Mallick at Dakshineswar when
his eyes focused on a painting of the Holy Virgin with
the Infant Jesus. He was filled with a Divine Emotion.
The faces that he was contemplating came to life, and
the rays of light that emanated from them entered into
his soul. This vision far exceeded his Muslim vision. (It
was his first encounter with Jesus, who in his view
became an incarnation of Love.) The vision was indeed
so potent that, carried away, he cried out: "O Mother,
what are you doing with me?" Shattering every barrier
of belief or religion, he was lifted into a new state of
ecstasy. Christ possessed his soul. For several days he
could not enter the temple of Kali. On the fourth day,
when he was walking in the Panchavati, he saw ap-
proaching him a man with beautiful eyes and a light
skin, utterly serene. When they were face to face, a
voice spoke in the depths of Ramakrishna's being:
"Contemplate Christ, who shed his heart's blood for
the redemption of the world and who suffered an
ocean of anguish for the love of man. It is he, the
Master, who is in eternal union with God. It is Jesus,
Love incarnate." And *The Gospel of M.* (page 34)
continues: "The son of Man kissed the Son of the
Divine Mother and was dissolved in Him."

The priest of Dakshineswar had "realized" his identity with Christ as, in turn, he had identified himself
with Kali, Rama, Hanuman, Radha, Krishna, *Brahman*, and Muhammad. Ramakrishna entered into
samadhi and into communion with *Brahman* with at-

tributes. He discovered that Christianity too was a road that led to the Awareness of God. Until the end of his life he believed that Christ was a Divine Incarnation, but not the only one. Buddha, Krishna, and Saitanya were among the others.

Having accepted the divinity of Buddha, he strove to find the likenesses between his teachings and those of the *Upanishads*. Without requesting formal initiation into religions other than his own, he profoundly lived their ideals. His vast love of God erased all religious barriers. Then he was to utter those famous words inscribed in *The Gospel of M.* (pages 35 and 135):

I have practiced all religions—Hinduism, Islam, Christianity—and I have also followed the paths of the various sects of Hinduism. . . . And I have found that it is the same God toward whom all are turned, along different roads. . . . You have to pass along these various roads in the practice of each religion once. Everywhere I see men who dispute in the name of religion: Hindus, Muslims, Brahmos, Vaishnavites, etc. But they do not stop to think that he who is called Krishna is also called Siva, and that he is also called Primal Force or Jesus or Allah! exactly like the single Rama and his thousand names. It is a pool entered by many *ghats* (stairs). From one, the Hindus draw the water in cruses and call it *jal;* from another, the Muslims draw the water in leather bottles and call it *pani;* from a third, the Christians draw it and call it *water.** Can we imagine that this fluid is not *jal*

* In English in the original.—Translator

❁

III

but *pani* or *water*? How absurd! The substance is one
under different names, and each man is looking for the
same substance; only the climate, the temperament, and
the name create difficulties . . .

He did not believe that any one religion could hold
the whole truth to the exclusion of the others. Now the
Christian, like the Jew or the Muslim, recognizes no
other revelation than his own. The problem of religious unity lies in these basic, irreducible oppositions.
But can there not be mutual respect? According to
Ramakrishna, every metaphysical concept calls for a
form in which to express itself, but it is impossible to
believe that only one such form exists. This is equally
true for the spiritual content, universal in nature, of
religion, which, even though it be presented in different terms and under a multitude of aspects, nevertheless remains identical with itself. Religions are special
expressions, limitations of the Transcendental Truth,
he said, which overflow or shatter their frames—or else
abandon them for new structures when the old ones
begin to stifle them.

He believed in the existence of God, a unique and
supreme principle of every faith, and that religions are
roads that take the believer to Him. It was his custom,
using a colloquial imagery, to say:

God is on the roof. It is a matter of climbing up to Him.
Some use a ladder, others a rope, or a stone stairway, or a

"A pool has many *ghats* . . ." (Upjaïn)

112

bamboo pole; still others make their way up in their own fashion. What is essential is to reach the roof. It makes little difference whether you have chosen this method or that. What you must not do is to try several at the same time; try them in succession. When you have found God, you are on the roof . . . and then you recognize that one can take different roads in order to arrive there. In no event should you believe that the other roads do not lead to God. They are other paths toward the same roof. Let each man follow his own path. He who genuinely and ardently searches for God, peace be upon him. Surely he will find Him. You may say as often as you like that there are many errors and superstitions in some other religion; I will reply: "Let us assume this to be so. Every religion includes errors. Every man thinks that his watch tells the correct time. It is sufficient to be ardent in one's love of God. It is enough to love Him and to feel oneself drawn to Him. Do you not know that God is our inner guide?" (*The Gospel of M.*, page 112.)

Depressed by his protracted austerities, Ramakrishna was eager to breathe the pure air of his native place. He went to Kamarpukur in 1867. There he was reunited with his young wife, Sarada Devi, who was now fourteen and whose spiritual growth amazed him and enabled him to make her his pupil when she requested it. Her heart swelling with gratitude, the new pupil called her joy "indescribable."

❀

Charity

But Sarada's *guru* could not stay long in Kamarpu-kur. At the beginning of 1868 he had to accompany Mathur Babu on several pilgrimages that Mathur had to make. The group of some 125 pilgrims went first to Benares, the holy city, that "compressed mass of spir-ituality," and then to the junction of the Ganges and the Jumna; shortly afterward the pilgrims visited Vrindaban. At Vaidyanath in Behar, when Rama-krishna saw how miserable the people were, emaciated, looking like so many skeletons in their abject poverty, Swami Nikhilananda tells us (*The Gospel of M.,* page 35), he asked his rich protector to succor these un-fortunates and give them clothing. Mathur replied that his entire fortune would not be enough to ease such terrible hardship. The priest of Kali announced that he wanted to share the lot of these poor people and that he would stay among them. Mathur bowed to Ra-makrishna's invincible will and agreed to make great sacrifices in order to improve the living conditions of these wretched people.

Later Ramakrishna accompanied Mathur on a visit to the latter's estates. Together they saw how poor the harvest had been, and again the problems were the same for those who could not pay their rent. Here again the priest of Kali prevailed on Mathur Babu to give help and to offer a gift to all these sufferers by

❈

"You are only the overseer for the Divine Mother . . ." (Rishkesh)

canceling their obligations. Mathur Babu objected at first, but Ramakrishna replied: "You are only the overseer for the Divine Mother. These people are her tenants. You ought to spend the Mother's money. When they suffer like this, how can you refuse to help them?" (*The Gospel of M.*, page 36.) And Mathur obeyed.

Ramakrishna's sympathy for the unfortunate derived from his conception that God is in every being. In his case it was not a matter of humanism or philanthropy, for the service of mankind was solidly bound to the service of God on the same basis as worship and therefore love for one's neighbor ought to be an essential. Hence he was to tell Swami Shivananda one day during a state of hyperconsciousness: "*Jiva* is Siva (the living being is God). Who can speak of showing him pity? Do not pity him but serve him, serve him by looking on man as God!" Vivekananda was also present. Hearing these observations gravid with thought, he said to Shivananda: "I have heard a lofty word today . . . I will proclaim its living truth to the world."

And Swami Shivananda concluded: "Whoever may seek the root of the innumerable works of service that have since been performed in India by the Ramakrishna Mission will find it here." (Rolland, *Life of Ramakrishna,* page 98.)

No barriers among men, no frontiers among religions—such was Ramakrishna's profound, unshakable conviction. The love of God should extend in all directions and the first duty is to keep it alive in one's heart like a permanent flame in spite of all ordeals.

The Master had to endure harsh tests, as well as deprivations and sacrifices, in the years that followed. A loss that especially grieved him was the death of his nephew, Akshay. He himself offered this account:

Akshay died before my eyes. But I was not affected by it. I stayed close to him and I watched over this man who was dying. It was like a sword snatched from its scabbard. I wanted to make this departure beautiful with dance and song and laughter. The body was taken away to be burned. But the next day, when I was still there (he pointed to the corner of the veranda that faced the sunset), I felt a horrible pang at the loss of Akshay, as if my heart were being twisted like a wet rag. It surprised

❁

me, but I recognized that the Mother was instructing me, giving me a lesson. I was not too concerned with my own body, much less than with those of my relatives. But my grief at the loss of this nephew was so keen that I sensed what it must be for a father to lose one of his dearest children. (Introduction to *The Gospel of M.*, page 40.)

In 1871 Ramakrishna suffered a fresh grief: his friend and protector, Mathur Babu, died. Five years later it was the turn of Sambhu Mallick, who had sustained Ramakrishna through many hardships. Ramakrishna's brother died in 1873 and his mother in 1876. This succession of bereavements left a painful mark on Ramakrishna's sensitive spirit, even though he better than anyone knew that the soul is immortal and death is mere illusion.

Those who are attached to earthly things dread death. But he who is not blinded by the world no longer takes notice of death. More than once, my vision intensified by meditation, I have stood at the border between the worlds and contemplated those two dwellings: life here and life beyond. . . . And was there no death that divided them? Then free yourself from your attachment to things; and immediately you will discover that life is One. That interruption in life that is called death does not exist. (Mukerji, *The Face of Silence,* page 107.)

Here again the saint of Dakshineswar crumbled the barriers, did not believe in them, did not see them. All that he saw was One Life, the Absolute in God.

Sarada Devi

It was in 1872 that Sarada made her first visit to her husband. She was no longer a child; she was eighteen years old, and her already mature mind had grasped Ramakrishna's mission as well as her own, which was to remain in the background. Since her husband's previous visit to her, four years earlier, and in spite of her keen desire to be with him in Dakshineswar, she had had the wisdom to wait patiently to be summoned by him.

But, when she heard the rumors of the strange behavior of Ramakrishna, who was said to have gone mad, Sarada was grieved and troubled, and she wondered whether she ought not to be with him. She refused to believe that so pure and perfect a man, as he seemed to her to be, could lose his senses. She resolved to set out for Dakshineswar.

Accompanied by her father and after a most arduous journey (she was stricken by fever along the way), she arrived at the garden-temple and was immediately reassured. The Master greeted her warmly. Her fears entirely dissipated, she saw that the disturbing rumors were exaggerated gossip, and in all tranquillity of soul she was able to dedicate herself to the service of her husband.

In the face of the marital problem that was presented to him, the ascetic Sri Ramakrishna felt no embarrass-

❊

Sarada Devi

ment. At once he wanted to make his wife share the
lofty ideal that was represented by his life, and he
urged her to remain with him in a purely spiritual
relation. He taught her that he regarded every woman
as the Divine Mother and that this was the only emotion that he could offer her. He added, however, thus

❧

revealing both his sense of responsibility toward her and the great sacrifice that he was prepared to accept: "If you desire to draw me into the world of Illusion, since I am your spouse, I am at your disposition." (Vivekananda, *My Master,* Volume IV, 1928, page 169.)

The generosity of the offer was met by a response worthy of the woman. Aware of her duty as a wife and eager to encourage her husband in his mission, Sarada left him free to lead the life that he preferred. Touched by the delicacy of his young wife's heart, Ramakrishna resumed with her the function that he had fulfilled in Kamarpukur, concerning himself daily with instructing her to the best of his ability both in her religious obligations and in her household duties, so that Sarada, vastly enriched by her husband's teaching and filled with a blissful serenity, observed: "It is as if a full measure of happiness had been poured into my heart." (*The Life of the Holy Mother, Sri Sarada Devi,* page 26.)

It was the same at Dakshineswar. In association with Sri Ramakrishna she acquired the habit of regular meditation. She learned to submit henceforth to religious disciplines faithfully followed, which, by contributing to the growth of her spiritual awareness, prepared her for the tasks that awaited her.

The tender respect that the young priest of Kali felt for Sarada's innocence and humility made it possible for her to understand her own duty better. One day,

❄

while she was massaging Ramakrishna's feet at his request, Sarada asked him: "How do you think of me?" He replied: "I think of you as the Divine Mother who is the Goddess of this temple—as the mother who bore me and who now lives in the *nahabat*. For me you are really the Divine Mother." (*The Life of the Holy Mother, Sri Sarada Devi*, page 33.)

Sarada's chief duty was that of cooking. The slightest deviation in diet affected the health of her husband, who had a delicate stomach. His food had to be prepared with great care. Sarada alone had the gift of cooking it exactly to the Master's taste.

The touch of humor that was so characteristic of Ramakrishna's mind appeared again when he asked his wife: "What does the word *wife* mean for a person like myself?" With a teasing smile he made his own response: "Don't you see? Let us suppose that she were not there: who would be able to prepare my meals exactly as they must be if I am to keep my health?" (*The Life of the Holy Mother, Sri Sarada Devi*, page 52.)

Whenever Sarada was away from Dakshineswar, the Master suffered stomach trouble, and often he sent after her to return quickly. The Holy Mother, as she was later to be known, lived in the *nahabat*, where her husband went once every day to see her; then he would tell her when she could go out, because Sarada remained invisible to all and went out only when she was certain that she would meet no one.

Ramakrishna's bedroom at Dakshineswar

At the time of her arrival at Dakshineswar her husband had allowed the young woman to serve him, and this she did with joy, but during the first six months of her stay he also permitted her to sleep in his room. Here is what Sarada said on this matter:

The Divine State into which it was his habit to plunge himself defies all description; when he was in ecstasy, he laughed or wept; sometimes he attained to the great *samadhi,* and then his whole body assumed the rigidity of a block of stone. I have often seen him remain an entire night like this. In the presence of the Divine I felt in myself a sacred horror, and I waited with anguish for the dawn, for in those days I was ignorant of all these matters. Once the *samadhi* was protracted beyond all meas-

❋

ure! In terror I sent for Hriday; he hurried to me and began to repeat the name of the Lord in the Master's ear. The result of this procedure was to recall Sri Ramakrishna to relative consciousness, but after this incident he understood my concern and he taught me some of the appropriate *mantras* that, depending on the nature of his *samadhi,* I had to murmur into his ear. To me this was a great relief, for I observed that the Master regained his normal consciousness whenever I pronounced these sacred names. Nevertheless, I still went through long nights without sleep, because one could never know whether he was not suddenly going to enter into *samadhi.* He recognized, after a test lasting several months, that I should never be able to adjust myself to his mystic tendencies; therefore he asked me to go to the *nahabat* to sleep in solitude. (*The Life of the Holy Mother, Sri Sarada Devi,* pages 34–5.)

This pure-hearted woman, so devoid of selfishness, was to learn without the least artifice to efface herself unceasingly in order to be only the Master's silent, attentive shadow. Her modesty was so great that she never appeared before him without covering her face.

Practicing *japa,* meditation, every day, she repeated her *mantra* with the utmost zeal and obeyed all the secret instructions that Ramakrishna had given her. Soon she, who had never yet entered into *samadhi* before her arrival at the garden-temple, was herself to be plunged into it, and it transformed her inner life while she awaited the deep experiences that she was to have later as a result of the spiritual training that her *guru* gave her and that made it possible for her to attain the Divine Realization.

Altogether, Sarada spent approximately thirteen years at Dakshineswar, but she saw the Master only at meals, in spite of the very great affection that existed between them. He watched over her nonetheless, and he was unhappy and enveloped her in his solicitude when he knew that she was ill.

From the earliest days of their life together, Sarada was able to reply to her husband's question: "Do you want me to be trapped in *Maya*'s nets?" with these touching words of abnegation and real simplicity: "I have come only to help you to follow the path of the religious life." (*The Life of the Holy Mother, Sri Sarada Devi*, page 35.)

The mother of this great-hearted young woman one day told her son-in-law how grieved she was that her daughter could not know the delights of motherhood. Ramakrishna answered gently: "Do not torture yourself on this matter; your daughter will have so many children that she will grow weary of hearing herself called *mother* night and day." (*The Life of the Holy Mother, Sri Sarada Devi*, page 34.)

It is possible that full measure has not always been accorded to the important even if so limited place that the Holy Mother was able to gain in the life of her husband, who, however, was the first to pay tribute to Sarada's eminent virtues, virtues that he held in special esteem. He admitted later to his disciples that he had

❉

prayed to the Divine Mother that the spirit of his wife might preserve its total purity, and he saw as he lived with her that the Divine Mother had fully granted his prayer.

The young wife's spiritual transformation was accomplished by Ramakrishna's sanctity and the disciplines that he taught her from the moment of her arrival at the garden-temple. These various disciplines, which she conscientiously followed, made it possible for the priest of Kali to pay a splendid tribute to Sarada, the crown of the religious elevation that she had gained, and to recognize the real worth of conjugal union in man's religious evolution.

One May night—to be precise, May 25, the date for celebrating the adoration of the Divinity in the form of the Mother—the temple of Kali in Dakshineswar was specially prepared. It had been decorated with flowers in abundance, there was a vast crowd at the hour of worship, and Sri Ramakrishna beckoned to Sarada to sit in the chair reserved for the Deity. Thus he identified her with the Great Goddess herself and worshiped her according to the rites, for in the stead of the image of the Divinity he had placed the living image that was Sarada Devi.

Throughout the ceremony the Holy Mother was in a state of religious fervor that was so deep that, as soon as the worship was over, she entered into *samadhi* simultaneously with Ramakrishna. Thus their spiritual union was consecrated in this ceremony of *sodasi puja,* and it was many hours before they returned to normal consciousness. After the *samadhi,* Ramakrishna sang a hymn to the Great Goddess, and at her feet he laid his rosary and the fruit of his long *sadhana*—in other words, the realization of the great teaching of the *Upanishads.*

For the adorer of Kali this solemn act marked the triumph of the spirit over the body; for Sarada it was the symbol of her true participation in her husband's life. Banishing all personal motivation, she fulfilled her task with perfect humility. When, later, Sri Ramakrishna died, the burden of many of his responsibilities passed on to her. The spiritual internalization that the priest of Kali had aroused in Sarada's heart, which was converted into spiritual energy, made it possible for her to carry on her husband's ministry.

It was given to the Holy Mother to commune with one of those divine beings; in this way not only was she drawn into the current of spiritual awareness that swirled about her but she was to show future generations the road that they must thereafter take in order to easily obtain inner Realization. (*The Life of the Holy Mother, Sri Sarada Devi.*)

Sarada died in Calcutta in 1920 after having provided maternal support and help to innumerable children, as her husband had earlier predicted, and indeed she was able to grant the major initiation to some of her spiritual sons.

❁

This divine glory of Sri Ma (as she was known) is manifested in her village by the temple with the white dome and the golden pinnacles that now soars on the exact site of her parents' house, in which she was born. It is the only structure in stone. It can be seen from a great distance in that flat region, like a lighthouse among clusters of palm trees. A little cement wall cut by a door, a well, both as simple as those of any farm in France. A few stairs of red cement lead to the circular veranda that surrounds the shrine. Beneath the three white arches, in the depths of a large room, the marble of the altar glistens below a richly sculptured vault; there are a portrait of the Holy Mother, flowers, silks, and copper utensils for the ceremonials.

It is Lizelle Reymond to whom we are indebted for this evocative description of that little Bengali village, Jayrambati, where Sarada was born, a village only a few miles from that other village, Kamarpukur, that was the birthplace of Gadadhar who was to become Sri Ramakrishna.

No trace remains of the mud hut with the thatched roof in which Sarada spent her childhood, but it would appear that all the houses of Jayrambati are alike.

Sarada Devi's house at Jayrambati

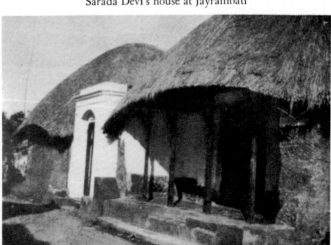

The Mother

Lizelle Reymond continues in her beautiful, moving description, which has the atmosphere of a fairy tale:

On each side of the temple stairway a banana tree has been planted—the pure plant that usually announces that God is visiting the house thus marked. Perhaps more than anything else, these banana trees indicate what now distinguishes Sri Ma from other village women. She has become the center of the missionary work of the monks who have established a homeopathic dispensary and, somewhat farther, outside the village, a school for the whole district. Sri Ma is the soul of the adoration of all her believers, she is the "Mother," *shakti* made manifest in a manner both personal and impersonal at the same time. (*Sri Sarada Devi and Sri Ramakrishna in Their Villages*, from *The Three Lotuses*, page 6.)

The humble little girl of Jayrambati, "who wept often when she was alone," but who had the capacity to sacrifice herself totally, day after day, with so pure a heart and in so modest a fashion, to the service of her Lord, has become a goddess "clad in silk woven with gold" and surrounded by flowers and lights in her white marble niche in the temple of Jayrambati.

Brahmasamaj

During the nineteenth century two great religious movements played important parts in the spiritual rebirth of India. These were movements that came into be:ng within Hinduism itself, as others have incessantly done through the centuries, testifying by these vigorous reactions to the permanent vitality of the Hindu religion.

The first of these two, *Brahmasamaj,* which means the doctrine of a single God, or Unitarianism, was an aspiration toward religious Unity. It was founded by a man endowed with an inspired mind and universal capacities, Ram Mohun Roy (1774–1833). Thanks to his knowledge of numerous Eastern and Western languages, which gave him access to all the currents of contemporary thought, he was a pioneer in the nascent universalism. Although he came of an orthodox Brahmin family, he had been steeped since childhood in the purest Sufism, while at the same time showing great sympathy for Christianity. Then, eager to study Buddhism, he went to Tibet and remained there for a considerable time. But he went home disillusioned. Accepting from Christianity its moral content and its ethic, he rejected the divinity of Christ; no longer did he accept the Hindu Incarnations or *Avatars*. In spite of his fidelity to the monotheism of Islam, he always turned back to the *Vedas,* the unshakable foundation of his mystic inspirations.

Brahmasamaj, which he created in 1828, was dedicated to the worship and "adoration of the Eternal, the Inaccessible, the Immutable Being who is the Author and the Preserver of the Universe." (*The Gospel of M.,* page 40.)

Theistic, independent, rationalistic, Ram Mohun Roy gave no allegiance to any particular orthodoxy but called himself a "unitarian." He adored God ONE and Indivisible. He sought to restore the true spirit of the *Vedas* by studying the Gospels. In fact, he wrote a book on Christianity.

His travels, his studies, and his rebellion endowed his native genius with an intellectual potency, a spiritual richness, and a human knowlege whose scope made him a rare personality.

Brahmasamaj, the House of God, was consecrated to the worship of the single *Brahman* without another, the Eternal Being who should be adored under no name or title or designation specifically employed by any man or group of men for any particuar being. (*The Gospel of M.,* page 40.)

Open to everyone without distinctions as to caste, nation, or religion, *Brahmasamaj,* pursuant to the desire of Ram Mohun Roy, was to be a universal church of prayer, "in which no religion was outraged or treated with contempt." A kind of foreshadowing, one might say, of the World Congress of Faiths created in England before the Second World War, which progresses gradually in the world as the affirmation of an attitude of mind, of understanding, and mutual respect among different religions whose basic principle is the "spirit of charity" that ought to bring men closer instead of dividing them.

It is difficult to find a more precise way of defining the monotheistic doctrine that was to serve as the foundation of Ram Mohun Roy's universal religion. Emancipated from any narrow nationalism, he sought to foster India's spiritual and social progress. He was much assisted in his efforts toward Unity by the very liberal tendencies of the early governors general of India, in particular Warren Hastings, whose prophetic observation was often quoted later: "The writings of the Indian philosophies will survive when British domination in India will long since have ceased to exist." (Rolland, *Life of Ramakrishna,* page 114.)

This great citizen of the universe in his own fashion, Ram Mohun Roy, died in 1833 in England, to which he had been invited to attend the debate in the House of Commons on the renewal of the East India Company's charter. He was buried in Bristol, and his tombstone bears this epitaph: "A conscientious and consistent believer in the Unity of the Divinity, he consecrated his life with complete devotion to the worship of the one Holy Spirit." (Rolland, *Life of Ramakrishna*, page 115.)

The seed had been planted; it was to take root and, in India and elsewhere, to bear this same fruit of universal faith.

When Ram Mohun Roy died, he was succeeded as the head of *Brahmasamaj* by the Tagores. Devendranath Tagore (1817–1905) a great mystical figure and the father of the poet, Rabindranath, was its real organizer. The nobility of his character and the beauty of his appearance, as well as his delicate sensibilities, earned him a very special respect among the young people, who admired him. Devendranath Tagore provided the orientation for the Movement's faith and ritual. An implacable enemy of image worship, he was equally vigorous in battling the Christian ideas that were infiltrating into *Brahmasamaj*.

He derived his entire inspiration from the *Upanishads*. Under his influence the *Brahmo* believed that only the ONE existed, the Supreme Being who had created the universe out of nothing, out of the void, and that He was the God of Truth, of Infinite Wisdom, of Goodness and Power, the Eternal and the Omnipotent, the ONE without another. It is the duty of man to believe in Him,

❁

to adore Him, and to do His Will. This is how his merit will make him find salvation in the other world. (*The Gospel of M.,* page 41.)

In 1852 a disciple of Devendranath Tagore, Keshub Chandra Sen, became the leader of *Brahmasamaj.* Unlike his predecessors, he was not a member of the aristocracy; he came from the upper middle class of Bengal. Educated in an English school and never having learned Sanskrit, he broke rather quickly with the current practices of the Hindu religion.

In spite of their mutual affection, discord between him and Devendranath seemed inevitable. Tagore was combatting Christianity, whereas Keshub had borne an indisputable Christian impress since his youth. Keshub's faith in Christ, indeed, constituted a problem complex enough to unsettle him and to raise painful inner doubts that often made him incomprehensible to his associates, in spite of that "limpid sincerity" that was later to be praised by Sri Ramakrishna, who admired him and held him in real affection as long as he lived. Each was influenced by his religious and social contacts with the other, although, it is true, the influence was not the same in both cases. When Keshub endeavored to introduce Christ, toward whom he ever more strongly inclined, into *Brahmasamaj,* the rupture with Devendranath Tagore occurred. Keshub assumed the leadership of a new Indian *Brahmasamaj,* and Devendranath remained at the head of the first, which he renamed *Adisamaj.* This separation was an agony

❄

Keshub Chandra Sen

for disciple and Master alike, but Keshub, who had brought about the scandal of this schism, had to withstand bitter rancor, for he was accused of having shaken the foundations of the Movement by seeking to broaden its spirit.

After a long moral crisis followed by a period during which he thought that he heard the summons of God, Keshub spent many hours singing sacred hymns with those who had remained loyal to him. Then he decided to visit England, where he had an important conversation with Queen Victoria. Afterward, having charmed many Britons with the simplicity of his language, the musicality of his voice, and, above all, his spiritual

❀

fervor, he went back to his own country. There he established new centers of *Brahmasamaj* and, on his first encounter with Sri Ramakrishna, he discovered the harmony of religions, which led to his acquiring a more liberal understanding of the gods and goddesses of the Hindu religion. Somewhat later he thought that he had been chosen by God to disseminate a new Law, "The New Dispensation," just as in his early youth, he claimed, he had had the direct experience of an inspiration sent from John the Baptist and Christ.

Believing in the universality of Christ's message, Keshub Chandra Sen too could have been called a link between East and West. Won over by Christian morality, which he had studied deeply, Keshub had asserted that "it is only in Christ, through the two principles of forgiveness and sacrifice of self, that Europe and Asia will be able to recapture their harmony and their unity." (*The Gospel of M.*, page 42.)

In 1878 Keshub's *Samaj* was split by a schism. Some disciples charged him with having infringed the principles of *Brahmo* by giving his daughter in marriage before she had reached the age specified in the laws of the Movement. Whether it was really for this reason or for some other, the group of dissidents founded the *Sadharanasamaj*, while Keshub remained at the head of the *Navavidhan*, a sect that was Christian in type.

An inevitable reaction from the old nationalist depths of India occurred as a result of all these events, and this was the second Movement of the late nine-teenth century in India from the religious point of view. Dayananda, who was born in the Punjab in 1824, founded a purely Indian *Brahmasamaj* in 1875. For fifteen years he traveled the holy places of his country as a *sadhu,* in the utmost poverty, in order to build his Association of the Aryas of India. His basic principles were the equality of the sexes and equal justice for all persons. *Brahmasamaj* had been an attempt at a church that would achieve the spiritual Unity of Orient and Occident, a kind of compromise with European culture that tacitly accepted Western superiority. *Aryasamaj,* on the contrary, directed by an aggressive Hindu *san-nyasin,* rejected Islam and Christianity. Dayananda resolved to combat and destroy all foreign influences established in India. By giving his ideas a universalist turn, he sought to beat back the Western rationalism that was modifying the depth of Indian philosophical conceptions. To him Christianity was a peril of the same type as Muhammad and the Koran.

Brahmasamaj had gained ground only in certain in-tellectual circles already tinged with Western culture, but *Aryasamaj* emerged as a potent, active force among the Indian masses. A dogmatic and intolerant move-ment, it preached the single path of the *Vedas* that leads to Truth. Sri Ramakrishna met Swami Dayan-anda only once, when the latter went to Bengal.

This was not the case with Keshub. It was in 1875 that his relations with Ramakrishna began. Keshub

❊

wanted to embrace everything at once—Christ, *Brahman*, the Gospels, the *Yogas*—and express this synthesis in the form of "The New Dispensation," or *Navavidhan*, but the Saint of Dakshineswar was satisfied to act it out with a smiling indulgence:

Do not talk about love for your brother! Love! Do not debate on doctrines and religions. There is only one. All rivers flow into the ocean. Go, and let others go! . . . The great torrent cuts its own bed in the slope—in accord with races and ages and souls. It is still the same water. Go, flow into the ocean. (*The Gospel of M.,* page 181.)

As for Keshub, he replied: "You shall honor and love all the ancients of the human family: prophets, saints, martyrs, philanthropists of all times and all countries without caste prejudice." (*The Gospel of M.,* page 181.)

Many visits by Ramakrishna to Keshub and by Keshub to Ramakrishna are recounted in Mahendra Nath Gupta's *Gospel.* The two friends' religious "views," however, were not identical. The Master, who had "realized" God in the quality of Pure Spirit and Pure Consciousness, also believed that God could assume all forms. Ramakrishna told Keshub one day:

It is absolutely true that God takes a human form to manifest Himself on earth, as in the case of Krishna, and it is also true that God can manifest Himself to His believers in varied forms. But it is equally true as well that God is without form. He is the Indivisible *Satchitananda:* Existence-Knowledge-Absolute Felicity. He has been de-

❁

138

scribed in the *Vedas* as being at the same time without form and able to assume forms. He is also described with and without attributes. Do you know what I mean? *Satchitananda* is like an infinite ocean. Intense cold changes the water into ice, which floats on the water in blocks of various shapes. In the same fashion, under the influence of *Bhakti* (love), one can apprehend the forms of God in the Ocean of the Absolute. These forms have meaning for those who are impassioned of God. But, when the sun of Knowledge rises, the ice melts and becomes water again, as it was before. The water above and the water below are everywhere the same water. That is why a priest in the *Bhagavad-Gita* says: "O Lord, You have a form and You are also without form. You walk before us, O Lord, in the form of a man, and yet You are described in the *Vedas* as being beyond the words of thought." (*The Gospel of M.*, pages 191 and 859.)

Keshub looked on the worship of images as idolatry; he was an orator and a writer, and he wanted to work for the regeneration of India by reforming her social laws. Ramakrishna had little interest in reading and asserted that he was barely able to write his own name. The sole purpose of life in his view was to "find" God and *adore* Him. But, in spite of these differences, the two men respected each other and sought each other out. Their meetings took place sometimes in the temple of Dakshineswar, sometimes in that of *Brahmasamaj*, where Ramakrishna's personal magnetism made itself felt among the believers in spite of certain reservations,

❋

the priest's attitude being deemed excessively austere. And yet, when Keshub in a ritual prayer recommended that his disciples adore God at every instant of the day, Ramakrishna remonstrated gently: "Adore Him twice a day with a burning heart. Say what you will really do. Why talk nonsense to the Infinite?" (Mukerji, *The Face of Silence,* page 365.)

Similarly Ramakrishna reproached Keshub for the endless enumeration of God's perfections and gifts:

Does a father tell his son: "O my Father, you have so many houses and so many gardens, so many horses"? It is natural for a father to put his resources at his son's disposal. If you think of Him and His gifts as of someone extraordinary, you will never become intimate with Him, you will never be able to draw near to Him. So think of Him as your nearest friend and He will reveal Himself to you. . . . Don't you see that His Attributes that send you into ecstasies are making you idolatrous? . . . Images and other symbols are as valid as your Attributes.

And Ramakrishna said further:

Those who believe that God is without form will attain to Him as well as those who believe that He has forms. The only two things required are faith and renunciation of self. . . . (Mukerji, *The Face of Silence,* I, page 365.)

The adorer of Kali, knowing the nobility of his friend's heart, did not hesitate to contradict him and show him his errors in order to make the teaching given by *Brahmasamaj* less solemn and more true. He

also criticized Keshub for that fear of sin that he end-lessly discussed with his disciples.

One day [he said], a friend was reading a book on Chris-tianity to me and all that it dealt with was sin. Now the poor man who spends the whole day repeating that he is a sinner ends by becoming one. One ought to have such faith in God that one could cry out: "How, if I pray so ardently to God, can I still be a sinner? O Lord,

❀

certainly I have done evil things, but I will not do them again." And Sri Ramakrishna entered into *samadhi*. (*The Gospel of M.,* page 138.)

The priest of Kali never wearied of urging the repetition of the Name of God, the most efficacious prayer of all, a kind of *mantra* of mysterious power. And in addition he went on: "Call on God with intense ardor. Shout, weep. People shed floods of tears for their wives and children. They swim in tears for money, but who truly weeps for God?" (*The Gospel of M.,* page 83.)

It was not from the spiritual point of view, of course, that Keshub could teach Ramakrishna anything—on the contrary, it was Keshub who always received the word of enlightenment that he needed—but at this time the leader of *Brahmasamaj* enjoyed genuine prestige among the youth of Bengal, and through his intercession the saint of Dakshineswar was brought into contact with all this young generation that he did not know. He wanted to know it. He was passionately eager to have disciples in order to let them share the treasures of his experiences. It was among these young men, moreover, that he was to find some of his dearest spiritual sons, such as Naren and Rakhal, and others, too.

During his visits to the *Brahmasamaj* he could gauge the influence of modernism on Hindu thought and life, and he observed that the new generation of these young men was making a compromise between God and the world and was much more interested in the

Western philosophers than in its own prophets. Sri Ramakrishna was not much concerned by this, because in everything he saw God's hand. As he explained his ideas on the Divine to the students, he endeavored to broaden their spiritual horizons, urging them at the same time to accept of his teaching only what suited their tastes and their temperaments.

Keshub arranged meetings at Dakshineswar or boat trips on the Ganges or to Calcutta for his friend, all of which Mahendra described so vividly in his *Gospel* that even after so many years they are singularly alive. They show us Ramakrishna surrounded by believers incessantly putting questions to which he replied with his usual gentleness, accompanied at times by teasing criticism.

One day when Keshub asserted with great fire that he wanted to clean the impure sky of Hinduism, protesting vehemently against the excess of abuses, Ramakrishna replied:

You see, Keshub, this impure sky, as you call Hinduism, could not possibly be cleaned by invective. . . . That would change only the appearance of things; it would be powerless to better the reality of them. Real progress is brought about by him who blesses. Will you be able to launch on us the wave of benedictions that will overflow and transfigure all the shores of your life? You are a man of learning, Keshub, you can teach us what has been accomplished in this world by men who were Incarnations of God.

❁

As Keshub catalogued the perfections of Buddha, he concluded: "His vast gift of sympathy, his unbounded charity, and his austere moral purity gave all those who came into contact with them the radiance of better and nobler men. Is that what you call the 'benedictions' of the man-God who transforms the world? is that what you call the Being?"

"What other name could we give that power that lives in the Incarnations of God?" the priest of Kali replied.

"Ah, dear Master," Keshub cried, "you have caught me in a trap. I feel that you are right: only the God who is within us can awaken the God who is within others." (Mukerji, *The Face of Silence,* page 101.)

Ramakrishna added further that the soul of such a person becomes the chalice of his holiness:

Whatever he does to others, he makes them better, them and their basest dreams. And men, in amazement, pay him homage by calling him an Incarnation of God. Like God, he makes everything that he touches pure and true, and what he creates will always be immune to the ambushes of time. (Mukerji, *The Face of Silence,* page 104.)

When Keshub became ill, the saint of Dakshineswar often went to visit him and spoke to him at length about God. He knew that Keshub had little time left to live, and on his last visit he told him that the Master

A branch of the Ganges near Dakshineswar

❦

145

Gardener handles a rosebush forcefully in order to make it produce its finest flowers. He prunes it. "You too, Keshub, will be transplanted soon, because the Gardener expects the most magnificent burgeoning from you!" (Mukerji, *The Face of Silence,* page 105.)

A short time later Ramakrishna was informed of his friend's death, and he felt that he had lost half of himself.

The Final Years

Unlike the majority of biographies of illustrious men, the life of Sri Ramakrishna affords no collection of outside events that played a decisive part or exercised a particular influence on his thought. On the contrary, it might be said, his life is the muted accompaniment of the purely inner story of an exceptional soul and its spiritual steps toward the Absolute.

This priestly life, the mystic amplitude of which presents an almost supernatural character, was lived in its entirety on the bank of the Ganges, in the temple of Dakshineswar, to the regular rhythm of prayers and of adoration and the accomplishment of religious rituals.

Thus months and years were spent in glorifying God, in singing His praises and His sacred Name. The conversations with disciples or friends were the major daily incidents apart from the ritual. Two days a week

❊

Ramakrishna in 1881

were assigned to private visits, during which the Master
gave instruction to young men destined to become
monks, or else received strangers attracted by his saint-
liness. Certain privileged disciples often remained into
the evening and spent the night with him. They could
see him rise at dawn to pray to the Divine Mother in
his soft voice.

❊

One day in 1884, when Ramakrishna happened to be alone, he entered into *samadhi*. There was no one to hold him up or guide his steps, and so he fell and broke a bone in his left arm. This apparently commonplace accident had a certain effect on his spirit, for the pain was such that it prevented the Master from leaving his body again. There was no more ecstasy for him who unceasingly had escaped from the World of Names and Forms. He took this ordeal as an opportunity for a better understanding of the degree to which he was an instrument of Kali, the Great Goddess, and for learning that his mission was not to be accomplished solely in the spirit but also, on the contrary, with the collaboration of his human envelope, body and soul. Perceiving that God shows Himself in unforeseeable fashion in the phenomenal world, through good men and bad, he rejoiced to see the divine influence at work in the relative world. This was his prayer: "O Mother! Do not leave me without feeling, do not make me an ascetic, hard of heart; leave me in communication with men." (*The Gospel of M.,* page 74.)

The first symptoms of the illness that was to bring about his death appeared in April, 1885. He was suffering from an inflammation of the throat; long conversations and protracted ecstasies aggravated his pain. Many visitors were pouring into Dakshineswar. The Master refused to avoid the fatigue that his customary night and day conversations caused him. He enjoyed no rest, but, like St. Francis of Assisi, he sang to forget

❁

his sufferings even as he continued to lavish his help on every visitor who came to consult him. He cried: "Let us leave the body to concern itself with its illness, but, O my soul, remain forever in Divine Felicity." (*The Gospel of M.*, page 71.)

A throat hemorrhage led to a diagnosis of cancer. Taken to Calcutta for treatment by a prominent homeopath, Dr. Sarkar, Ramakrishna was established at Syampukur in a private house and surrounded by his disciples, who set up a regular schedule for attending him in turn. The disease spread. Feeling that his end was near, the Master gave his final instructions to Narendra in order that his message might be spread abroad after his death.

Sarada, whom everyone loved, took care of her husband, herself preparing his meals and his medicines and praying constantly. Sri Ramakrishna's own spiritual fervor had invested all those around him. Each person's devotion became a religious discipline in itself. Certain disciples (Girish in particular) regarded their *guru*'s disease as a means of attaining an undefined but higher goal, perhaps desired by the Divine Mother in order further to instruct his intimates and his disciples. Narendra and a few others believed simply that the Master's body, being a material thing, must like all material things be subject to physical laws.

The illness grew worse. At times the pain was unbearable. Ramakrishna now could take only liquid nourishment. While his face shone with joy, he grew

❁

more and more emaciated. Yet he welcomed everyone with a radiant smile. The more ravaged the body, the more it was inhabited by the Spirit.

He was moved to a more spacious house in Cossipore, in the middle of a garden of flowers and fruits. It was there that he lived his last months. His twelve disciples were with him. Latu, who followed no discipline because "service" was his own religion, entirely forgot his own rest and food in serving his Master.

It was suggested to Ramakrishna that he pray to the Mother to cure him, or at least to ease him. He replied that he could not pray for his body. "Do it for our salvation," his disciples begged. The ailing man murmured: "I will try. But I will do all that I can for you before I go." (*The Gospel of M.,* page 69.)

There was an improvement early in January and he was even able to stroll in the garden; then, seeing his disciples gathered round him, he said to them: "I bless you all; be illumined." They knelt at the feet of their *guru.* Each received a special blessing, and each, they all confided later, experienced something ineffable.

The Master, who had selected Narendra as his spiritual heir and the executor of his work, the guide for all, told him: "I am turning over these young men to your charge. See that they develop their spirituality and remain here." (Introduction to *The Gospel of M.,* page 70.)

Toward the end Ramakrishna made a revelation to his most intimate disciples: "I see that God has become

❈

every object. Men and animals are the framework
covered with flesh, but it is He who moves through
their brains and their limbs." (Introduction to *The Gospel of M.,* page 70.) Seeing that Latu was resting his
head on the palm of his hand, Ramakrishna said: "To
me that is the Lord sitting in that position." His most
trivial remarks were tender and moving. Like a mother
he looked at Narendra and murmured: "If this body
could endure longer, many other souls would be en-
lightened. But the Mother has decided otherwise."
Touching his chest, he added: "There are two beings
here: one is she and the other is her devout servant. O
soul, forget the body and be immersed in God." (*The
Gospel of M.,* page 61.)

During his last days he taught that *Brahman* is
always free, the three *gunas* are in it but it is not
affected by them, just as the wind that carries a scent
remains without odor. *Brahman* is the Infinite Being,
Infinite Wisdom, Infinite Mercy. In it there is no
disappointment, no misery, no illness, no death, no
growth, no decline. The Transcendent Being and Being are one and the same thing. There exists only the
indivisible ONE: the Absolute.

Narendra was meditating in concentration at the
Master's bedside. Suddenly he lost consciousness and
experienced *nirvikalpa-samadhi,* the realization of the
soul incarnate, of its unity with the Divine. He remained thus for a long time. When he had regained
only a part of his waking consciousness, he could not

manage to find his body. "Where is my body?" he cried. Gopal came in then. But Ramakrishna interrupted: "Leave him in this condition a little while. He has tormented me enough to achieve *samadhi.*" (*The Gospel of M.*, page 71.)

Bathed in indescribable peace, Narendra regained consciousness completely and his Master told him that the Mother had shown him *all* that he ought to know, but that he must keep this revelation for himself. A few days later, Naren again went into *samadhi.* He felt that he was being pervaded by a subtle force. When he woke, he saw Ramakrishna weeping, and the Master told him: "Now I have given you everything that I possessed. I am now no more than a poor *fakir;* I have nothing left. Through this power that I have transmitted to you you should do much good in this world, which you will not leave until your work has been finished." From that moment on, everyone knew that the Master was alive in his disciple. Some doubt persisted in the disciple himself. "Unless he says it is so, I dare not accept him as a Divine Incarnation." Reading his thought, Ramakrishna confided to him: "He who was Rama and Krishna is now in this body: Ramakrishna, but not in the Vedantic sense." Naren bowed deeply, ashamed that he had doubted. (*The Gospel of M.*, page 72.)

On August 15, 1886, the Master's pulse became irregular and his breathing difficult. About midnight he said again to Naren: "Take care of these boys." Then,

❀

152

three times, he cried the name of Kali. At one o'clock in the morning of August 16, his face radiant with a smile, he died. The ultimate ecstasy had begun.

As she was putting on her widow's garments, Sarada heard, in a flash of revelation: "I have merely gone from one room into another." (*The Gospel of M.,* page 73.)

3

The Teaching of Ramakrishna

Mahendra Nath Gupta asserted in his *Gospel* that his *guru*

> was a man like other men outwardly, wearing neither special garments nor a particular symbol, but inside he was very profound and difficult to understand. Beneath his natural spontaneity one discovered an astonishing synthesis of knowledge, love, and renunciation. (*The Gospel of M.*, page 505.)

The Master, who never wrote, read no books. "He

had them all at the tip of his tongue," Brinda, his serving woman, said. (*The Gospel of M.,* page 78.) One day when a disciple was amazed to hear him reply in a strikingly clear fashion to a metaphysical question, Ramakrishna said: "I have not read, but I have listened to those who do read. I have made a garland of their diverse knowledge and worn it round my neck until I laid it at the feet of my Divine Mother." (Introduction to *The Gospel of M.,* page 33.)

The loftiness of the saint's spiritual level and his tremendous power of assimilation gave him a knowledge that exceeded anything that can be learned from books. How is it possible not to recall the words of the Christian Gospel: "First seek the Kingdom of God, and the rest shall be given to you in abundance."

The *Guru*

Sri Ramakrishna in no way looked upon himself as a teacher, but rather as an obedient servant desirous of accomplishing the Divine Will. It was only on this ground that he occasionally expressed the thought of being the *guru,* the father, the friend of the young men who surrounded him and who questioned him. He felt that he ought to arouse the life of the soul in

The Panchavati

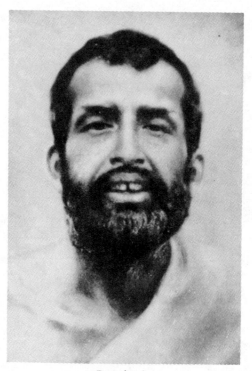

Ramakrishna

them and stimulate it. He sought above all to communicate to them his burning love of God.

There was no dogmatism in this Master. He instructed his disciples in intimate conversations that were part of the pattern of his days, between his religious duties and his hours of worship, and he carried on these talks to the limit of his energies in order to distribute untiringly the treasures of his wis-

❁

dom and of his experiences, always placing himself, with wise kindness, on the level of his questioner. The gift of second sight that he possessed made it possible for him to evaluate immediately the potentialities and the limitations of his companion. Then he knew how to prepare the ground and what fruits to expect from it. Thanks to this infallible discernment, each encounter made him behave differently. He was a remarkable fisher of souls.

It was by means of a subtle, indefinable influence, rather than any act, that he attracted his disciples. He fascinated them—all of them were aware of that—by the light that shone in his face, that face that blazed when he spoke to them of God.

Remakrishna had not evolved any system of teaching. It was his habit to say that one must never preach, but intensely *live* what one believed, and that example was the best lesson that one could give. He excelled in it and he lived his own faith with absolute genuineness.

The purpose of spiritual discipline is to sing the Name of God and His Glory in order to realize Him. A man attains this end when he discovers that his real Self is in himself. The object of *sadhana* is to obtain this result. That is why one assumes a body. One needs this mold of clay until the image of gold has been granted; but, when the image has been made, the mold of clay is discarded. God is not only within us. He is at the same time within us and outside us. (*The Gospel of M.,* page 521.)

After his ardent prayer to the Divine Mother to send

Mahendra Nath Gupta, the man
who handed down his guru's gospel

him disciples, they came one after another, forming
around him a circle of intimates that was to surround
him until his death. To each of them his presence—for
an irresistible force emanated from him—represented a
lesson and an enlightenment. These young men, even
while they looked upon him as a comrade because of
his gentle simplicity and his gaiety, respected him at
the same time and even feared him. They knew their
Master's amazing power to sweep away frivolous
thoughts, when these arose spontaneously in them during the conversation, and to transport his disciples
suddenly to a region that admitted neither weakness
nor compromise. Torn out of themselves, as it were, by

this rapid elevation of spirit, they discovered the divine ideal in its total purity. Overwhelmed, they preserved its ineffaceable stamp forever.

They were ready then for the total renunciation that their *guru* demanded of those who were destined to become monks. He did not urge so arduous a course on the others. But he demanded that everyone observe hours of meditation and prayer every day.

Sri Ramakrishna liked to use parables for the expression of his thoughts, selecting concrete, living images borrowed from nature, the stars, plants, and animals, in order to make the verities of the *Sanatana-Dharma* more easily understandable. In this he resembled the cosmic poetry of the *Vedas,* which draw their splendid figures from the moon, the sun, wheat, salt, or, sometimes, the human voice.

The teaching of the priest of Kali had always the same point of departure:

How to find God? As long as you are unable to say: "O God, You and You alone are real," you will not be liberated from the world of phenomena. The whole of creation is the Universal Form of God, but it is in man that God's manifestation is strongest, and stronger still in souls that are pure. The essential thing is to cultivate devotion to God above all else.

Naren was to sing unceasingly: "O Mother, make me mad for You. What need have I of reason or knowledge?" And his *guru* added:

❀

What is the point of counting the trees and the branches in the orchard of God? You have come to eat mangoes, to rejoice in all that God gives you in His orchard, to glorify Him for His creation. Do so and be happy. The purpose of human birth is to love God. Achieve this love and live in peace . . . God will teach you in the fullness of time what you should especially know. Have faith in the Divine Mother and remember that God can be found only through total renunciation. Follow the instructions of your *guru* step by step and you will find God. Otherwise you will have to be born and reborn. (*The Gospel of M.,* page 509.)

So lucid in his thinking, the Master abstained from all syncretism, all eclecticism. "Each of the devout," he declared, "should believe in the form of devotion that is suited to him. The bee buzzes only until it has settled on the flower. It becomes silent when it begins to ingest the nectar." (*The Gospel of M.,* page 103.)

A superior intelligence is not compelled to restrict itself to abstraction; it operates constantly in everyday life and finds its applicability there. A rather striking aspect of Ramakrishna's personality led him to take an interest in the most modest areas of existence. And he taught his disciples that the slightest gesture has its own importance: in connection with all others, it forms part of the person's spirituality. The same spirit should govern everything. Because he lived constantly in the presence of God, his attention was always perfect. He called on his disciples for the same attention:

❁

The Teaching of Ramakrishna

Without attention there is no concentration, and without
concentration there is neither intelligence nor spiritual
life. It is the power to apply oneself to the most trivial
things with the same concentration that is given to the
most important that makes it possible one day to attain
to *samadhi*. (Swami Siddheswarananda, *Bulletin of Cultural Activities,* No. 20.)

He also recommended to his spiritual sons that they
always adapt themselves to the varied circumstances
existing about them. He was forever setting the example. Able to identify himself at the same time,
without contradiction, with a divine form or with a
believer in another religion, he resolved the oppositions
within himself, always remaining at the center of the
position that he had chosen. He refused to embrace the
slightest prejudice of nation, race, caste, or individual
way of life, asserting that, in order to understand the
characteristics of a people or a country, one must first
of all *come out of* one's own person. On this point, too,
his conduct was exemplary. It is impossible to find any
instance of intolerance in him.

During a conversation with a disciple, Ramakrishna
said:

Do you know why God assumes incarnations? Because
through the human body His words can be heard. Only a
tiny fragment of Him is made manifest. God spoke to
me one day. I saw Him under the banyan tree, coming
from the Ganges. For three days I wept without interruption. He showed me what is in the *Vedas*, the

163

Puranas, and the other Scriptures. On another day He showed me the *Maya of Mahayaya:* a little light inside a dark room. It began to grow larger and in the end it invaded the universe. (*The Gospel of M.,* page 782.)

Having himself experienced in the *Vedanta* the three ways of union with Reality, he made them the bases of his habitual teaching. Let us recall here that the first is the dualist position, the second is that of modified dualism, or *vishitadvaita,* and the third is nondualism, or *advaita.* These three great philosophical systems, not contradictory but complementary, corresponded, in the view of the priest of Kali, who "saw" God with and without form, to the varying aspirations of individuals. To the Master they represented the three great stages of man's progress in his ascent toward the Absolute.

Bhakti

For the average person, the captive of tangible things, dualism is more accessible than the difficult abstraction of nondualism, *advaita.* There the philosophical position is stated thus: "O Lord, when I am conscious of my body, my relation with You is that of the servant toward his master." (*The Gospel of M.,* page 782.) The persistence of the self, or of a mere vestige of it, makes it possible to rejoice in the Presence of God and to love Him. It would be impossible to savor the Divine Beatitude without making a distinction between God and self. The ideal of the *bhakta* consists in the adoration of the personal God, the omnipotent God who, in His quality of Consciousness, penetrates everything. For the *bhakta* who accepts all states of consciousness, the waking state is real. He regards the world not as unreal but as the manifestation of the power and glory of God, who has created everything: stars, moon, mountains, etc. God is within us, in our hearts, but He is also outside us. The most advanced *bhaktas* believe that God Himself has become all things, the twenty-four principles of the universe, and all living beings.

This attitude of *Bhakti,* so dear to Ramakrishna, who asserted that it was in his nature to see the form of God, seemed of prime importance to him:

Who will ever be able to know God through reasoning? Even the reading of the six *darçanas* would not suffice. One must sing the Name of God and His glory. One can be set free of this life when one believes that God is the author of everything that is. The Will of God is exercised in everything, even in the little movement of a leaf. (*The Gospel of M.,* page 94.)

In order better to serve the Divine Purposes, the Great Goddess, Kali, to whom Her priest prayed constantly, allowed a trace of "self" to survive in him; according to his mood, he spoke of it as the self of Knowledge, the self of Devotion, or the self of the servitor. Occasionally Ramakrishna spoke of his *mature* self in contrast to his immature, or *green,* self, a prey to the world of women and gold.

❊

He whose soul is *green,* still bound by many ties, identifies himself with his body, his family, his possessions, wealth, and the world; but the *mature* self, illumined by Divine Knowledge, knows that body and family and all the rest are illusory, unreal things, and Ramakrishna himself desired only a unique relation of love with God: the state of *Bhakti.*

> There is no need for much reading of the Scriptures. You would be inclined to argue and debate. What you gain by repeating the Name of God with love ten times is the very essence of the Scriptures. Be mad for God, truly be athirst for God, the Divine Intoxication. Love, the key to Knowledge, opens all doors. (Introduction to *The Gospel of M.,* page 38.)

In his beautiful book Romain Rolland very rightly lays great stress on the profound meaning that the word *devotion* assumes in India in connection with *Bhakti:* the impassioned gift of self offered, in however inadequate fashion, out of devotion. "That old word of Christian mysticism, *sacrifice,* must be brought back to life in its true meaning," Romain Rolland said (*Life of Ramakrishna,* page 103), appending this quotation from Ruysbroek the Admirable on the subject of inner sacrifice: "If we seek to belong to God through inner sacrifice, in the very core of our will and of our love we will feel . . . what might be called the effervescence of a living spring that leaps up into eternal life."

When he was expounding the second aspect of the *Vedanta* to his disciples, the Master said that this was

❊

the believer's prayer in this modified dualism: "When I am conscious of being the *jiva* (the individual soul), I feel as if I were a part of you," and he added that, when he practiced this, he saw God: "I have seen that He and the one who lives within me are one and the same person. A mere line divides the two in order that I may be able to rejoice in this divine felicity."

In the third position of the *Vedanta*, which Ramakrishna so quickly reached, the self totally disappears. This is the believer's prayer: "When I am conscious of being *atman*, I am but one with you."

But Sri Ramakrishna, who had known absolutely unique spiritual experiences and who had stood so often on the threshold between the two worlds, the Absolute and the relative, was not wont to say: "I am He." He preferred to put it in this fashion: "The waves belong to the Ganges, not the Ganges to the waves." (*The Gospel of M.,* pages 103 and 812.) All his teaching is embraced in this. Therefore this was his prayer: "O God, You are the Master, and I am your servitor . . . You are the Mother, I am your child. You are my Father, my Mother, You are All, and I am a fragment of You." (*The Gospel of M.,* page 134.) This text from the *Bhagavataphurana* could be applied to Ramakrishna:

The movement of a heart that, just as the water of the Ganges flows to the sea, is constantly drawn toward Me—Me, the refuge of all souls—by the sole desire to hear the tale of my virtues: that is the sign of the pure *Yoga,* of the devotion of the best of Spirits, disinterested devo-

❋

"Just as the waters of the Ganges flow to the sea . . ."

tion that is no longer discrete from Me. Without their adoration for Me, those who are motivated by it would not accept, even if it were offered to them, the happiness of living in the same world with Me, of having the same greatness, of being in my presence, of having the same form and being only one with Me. *Bhagavatapurana,* from the French translation by A. M. Esnoul. (III, 29, ii, *et seq.*)

❁

The Disciples

With the exception of Gopal, who was already old when he became acquainted with the Master and, after his wife's death, renounced the world in favor of spiritual retreat, all Ramakrishna's disciples were adolescents when they embraced the monastic life. In general they belonged to Bengali families of the middle class that in some instances had looked forward to brilliant careers for them. They themselves aspired only to live with their *guru* in the temple of Dakshineswar, at which they arrived with sound minds, virgin souls, and pure bodies. Ramakrishna adopted them as his children. Contact with him transformed them quickly. All were spiritually gifted, but their gifts were various. Later each in his own fashion would mirror the teaching of the Master, becoming a bearer of light wherever he might turn his steps. In spite of the great differences in their characters, they lived in an atmosphere of the greatest understanding.

LATU

A disciple unique of his kind, Latu was the first to establish himself at the garden-temple. Of obscure origin, he was born in the Behar and moved to Calcutta in search of employment. There he became a

❁

169

servant in the home of a wealthy physician, Ramachandra Dutt, who took him one day to visit the priest
of Kali, of whom Dr. Dutt was a loyal friend and
follower. Totally without education but rich in intuition, Latu was deeply stirred at the sight of the Master.
He saw his destiny, and his conversion was instantaneous. Under Ramakrishna's guidance, his spiritual gains
brought him long meditations, followed even by ecstasies; all his *guru*'s efforts to give him the rudiments
of schooling, however, were fruitless. Latu could not
learn. He liked only religious songs. The highest type
of servitor, after his Master's death he was to remain at
the monastery under the name of Swami Adbhutan-
anda, allied in particular with Turiyananda, a scholar
of scholars, who held him in special esteem because,
without any intellectual assistance, he had so quickly
gained the vision of God. It was Latu of whom Sri
Ramakrishna was one day to say to the group of his
disciples: "Many of you have had to wade through the
muddy waters of Knowledge in order to come to God,
but Latu has leaped over them like Hanuman." Latu
was the symbol of the servitor's perfect love. (Rolland,
Life of Ramakrishna, page 205.)

RAKHAL CHANDRA GHOSH

Keshub Chandra Sen was the first to make a public
announcement of Ramakrishna's sanctity. Visitors began to be attracted to the temple on the bank of the

❈

A group of disciples at the time of Ramakrishna's death

Ganges, and so it was that one day Manomohan Mitra wanted to introduce his brother-in-law, Rakhal Chandra Ghosh (Swami Brahmananda), to the priest of Kali. We have already seen* that Rakhal was recognized by Ramakrishna, who had glimpsed him in a mystic vision only a short time earlier. Born of Brahmin parents who lived in luxury, Rakhal had spent a large part of his time from his earliest youth in prayers and contemplation. He neglected his studies in the preparatory school in Calcutta and showed greater interest in a sports club in which he came to know Naren. They were of the same age and they were to meet again at the *Brahmasamaj* and then to form a deep attachment to each other under their *guru*, Ramakrishna.

* Cf. Introduction.

❧

Swami Brahmananda (Rakhal Chandra Ghosh)

After his first visit to Dakshineswar and some re-
proaches from his father when the latter observed his
son's assiduousness at the garden-temple, Rakhal was
very soon to establish himself in a filial relation with
his Master. Ramakrishna granted him many favors
that he refused to others; nonetheless he would not
have hesitated to rebuke him if Rakhal had deserved it.
Ramakrishna said of him: "Rakhal was born with an
intense love of God. Such a love, as a rule, is acquired
only through years of spiritual exercise or in the course

❁

of many lives." (Swami Prabhavananda, *The Eternal Companion, Brahmananda,* page 2.)

There was a certain time when Rakhal was carried away by a childish jealousy that made him feel that the other young men were receiving visible evidences of the Master's affection in which he did not share. He was soon cured of this, recognizing that his *guru* was everyone's *guru* and that he was completely capable of portioning out his regard to each according to his needs. Second only to Vivekananda, Rakhal was to be the epitome of Ramakrishna's spiritual son, and little by little he was to elevate himself to the summit of mystical life: therefore, after their Master's death, the other disciples called him their *Maharaj* (king). He was to govern the monastery, while Vivekananda was to embark on his journeys through the world.

In his book, *The Eternal Companion, Brahmananda,* Swami Prabhavananda relates that Sri Ramakrishna regarded Naren and Rakhal as members of the class of the "Always Perfect," born with their knowledge of God. Rakhal had the gift of reading in men's hearts and thus recognizing their most secret motivations. His *guru*, learning that Rakhal occasionally employed this power, rebuked him severely: "The man who concerns himself with occult powers becomes incapable of living in the presence of God. Pay no attention to these phenomena when they occur in you." (Swami Prabhavananda, *The Eternal Companion, Brahmananda,* page 11.) And he added: "It is easy to acquire occult powers, but very difficult to attain purity of heart; he who pos-

sesses that knows the true countenance of religion."
(Swami Prabhavananda, *The Eternal Companion,
Brahmananda,* page 11.)

After Ramakrishna's death, Rakhal, who had become Brahmananda, was to accomplish many pilgrimages and, as a wandering monk, to withdraw into
solitude at Vrindaban, where he was to live in a state of
constant ecstasy. Swami Subodhananda was to stand
watch over him. After many years of pilgrimages,
Brahmananda recognized that he had achieved his
purpose. The state of *samadhi* was virtually habitual
for him. "The fullness of God lives in my heart," he
used to say. He went back to the monastery, for now he
was forever established in the consciousness of God and
"prepared" to respond to the call of duty in this world:
"Our Master was the personification of supreme Love
and Devotion. I want to serve my brothers and mankind." He fulfilled this pledge as long as he lived.

SURESH MITRA

Suresh Mitra, whom Sri Ramakrishna liked to call
Surendra, was a disciple much loved by his Master. He
had received an English education and held an important position in a British mercantile company. Quite
proud of his atheism and his indulgence of his caprices,
he was inclined to some excess in drinking and he
valued nothing more highly than the pleasures of a free
life. Very much impressed, however, by the personality

of the priest of Kali and above all by his total relinquishment of his own will to God's, Suresh made the decision to renounce his bad habits. The Master had asked him: "When a man goes to an undesirable place, why does he not take the Divine Mother with him?" A few remarks skillfully uttered from time to time by Ramakrishna caused Surendra to enter on the spiritual path. He was one of those who assumed the financial burdens of Dakshineswar.

TARAK NATH GHOSAL

A lawyer's son, Tarak Nath Ghosal had evidenced a keen desire to "find" God since his youth. He too had been a member of the *Brahmasamaj,* but he had been

Swami Shivananda (Tarak Nath Ghosal)

unable to find there what he was seeking. During a gathering in Ramachandra's house he met the Master and was surprised to hear him speak of *samadhi,* a subject in which he had long been deeply interested. When he saw that day that Ramakrishna often entered this higher state of consciousness, he had an intense desire to meet the priest of Kali again, and he became a faithful guest at the garden-temple. His fervor earned him abundant graces, and he learned from his *guru* that God grants them to those whose tears shed on His behalf are sincere, for these tears forever erase the sins of earlier lives. Tarak was to take the monastic name of Swami Shivananda when he became abbot of the Order of Ramakrishna.

Baburam Ghosh

On Baburam Ghosh's first visit to Dakshineswar, when he was accompanied by Rakhal, the priest of Kali, following his usual custom, examined his physiognomy and was satisfied with the latent spirituality that he descried in it. At the age of eight Baburam had wanted to become a monk. And he had installed himself in a hut concealed by a thick curtain of trees. The sight of the Panchavati reawakened this memory of childhood. His heart was so tender that his *guru* thought that "he was pure even to his bones!" On the strength of bad advice, he asked the Master to help him to obtain a certain spiritual power, and he was told:

❋

Swami Premananda (Baburam Ghosh)

Have I not given you everything of what I have gained
during realizations carried out for the salvation of all
of you? Do not beg me for more, because you could
only create a gulf between us. Tighten your bonds with
me and you will have the key to all treasures. (*The
Gospel of M.*, page 60.)

Baburam was to become Swami Premananda.

SASHIBSHAN AND SARATCHANDRA CHAKRAVARTY

Sashibshan and Saratchandra Chakravarty were cous-
ins who had come under the influence of Keshub

and had been members of the *Brahmasamaj*. Sashi's direct speech had pleased Sri Ramakrishna, who had asked him: "Do you believe in God with or without form?" Sashi had replied that he was not yet certain of God's existence. But he was to assume the monk's robe later under the name of Swami Ramakrishnananda.

As for Sarat, he aspired not to see God in this or that form but to realize Him completely. He wanted to see Him in all living beings. The Master pointed out to him that this was the ultimate peak of asceticism, and Sarat declared that no realization other than this crown of religious experience could satisfy him. This delighted Ramakrishna. Sarat, who was to become Swami Saradananda, was to be the devoted, attentive disciple of the Holy Mother, the wife of his *guru*.

NITYA NIRAJAN SEN

Mahendra wrote that Nitya Nirajan Sen, later Swami Niranjananda, was a disciple with a heroic character. At the age of eighteen, when he was a medium in a spiritualist group, he was told by the priest of Kali that, if he believed in ghosts, he would become one, but, if he believed in God, he would become divine. "Which do you prefer?" Ramakrishna asked. Nirajan quickly severed all ties with spiritualism. He was of a very violent temperament; one day, when he was traveling to Dakshineswar by boat, he

❈

heard disparaging remarks about his *guru* from some of the passengers. In his anger he protested, and then he began to rock the boat, threatening to turn it over. When he told the story to Ramakrishna, the Master rebuked him for his incapacity to curb his anger.

JOGINDRANATH CHUDHURY

In contrast to Nirajan, Jogindranath Chudhury, the future Swami Jogananda, was lacking in courage; in circumstances like those on the boat, he remained silent and showed not the slightest disapproval of the slanderers. Apprised of this, his *guru* reproached him harshly. Thus the same treatment was given to two disciples who had behaved in opposite fashions. The one ought to master his excessively violent reactions; the other ought to arouse those of his that bordered on cowardice. The Master strove to develop in each of his disciples that quality that was lacking.

HARINATH CHATTOPADHYAYA

A very great disciple of the Master, Harinath Chattopadhyaya, well known under his monastic name of Swami Turiyananda, had had a precocious vocation. Leading a life of austerity from childhood, he bathed daily in the Ganges, cooked his own food after he had

❀

recited the *Gita*, and rose at dawn. In his eyes the priest of Kali represented the very Incarnation of the Vedantic Scriptures. Eager to follow the teachings of Sankara, he studied zealously and knew the *Patanjali-Yoga* by heart. His father was one of the greatest Sanskrit scholars of his time, and the son took his place whenever he was absent. Harinath could recite the *Upanishads* for hours. He was the marvel of all who heard him. "My father taught me everything," he would say, "and Ramakrishna did the rest." When he met his *guru* for the first time, he put this question to the Master: "Can every man know God?" When Ramakrishna replied: "Yes, if God is willing," Harinath was plunged into a profound meditation, for he remembered that Sankara, with his proud nature, had not failed to say after the Revelation: "I am part of You; and by the grace of Your Compassion I am One with You." (Cf. Mukerji, *The Face of Silence*.)

Hari hated women. He confided to his *guru* that he could not allow even little girls to come near him. Sri Ramakrishna rebuked him:

You speak like a fool. Why do you hate women? They are the manifestations of the Divine Mother. Look at them as if each were your own mother and you will never come under their evil influence. The more you detest them, the more you will fall into their snares.

Hari was to say later that these few words had been enough to change his attitude toward women completely.

❁

Swami Turiyananda (Harinath Chattopadhyaya)

The adorer of the Divine Mother, knowing Hari's passion for the *Vedanta* but not wishing one of his disciples to become a "hard-hearted" ascetic, asked him to practice the disciplines of the *Vedanta* but urged him to abandon the unreal in his life in order to pursue the real.

This is not easy, he said, adding: You must discover that the world is illusory, and this is not easy, especially when one studies alone. The Grace of God is all-powerful and necessary. Mere personal effort is insignificant. A man is a very small creature, after all, with very small

❊

powers. He can hope for the impossible, however, if he prays to God to grant him His Grace. (*The Gospel of M.*, page 62.)

Thereupon the Master began to sing a hymn of praise to God. Deeply stirred, Hari burst into sobs. About midway in his life he achieved an amazing synthesis of his ideal of the personal God and of impersonal Truth.

Akhandananda

He who was one day to be Swami Akhandananda, Ganghadhar Ghatak, lived the strict life of the *brahmachari,* dedicated to the study of the Holy Texts. This enabled him to join the intimate circle around the priest of Kali, who esteemed the very austere religious disciplines of his new disciple.

Hariprasanna Chatterji

He also initiated Hariprasanna Chatterji, the future Swami Vijnanananda, into the spiritual life. Obedient to the counsels of his *guru,* the disciple followed them as long as he lived, remembering this one in particular: "Even if a woman is pure as gold and rolls on the ground for love of God, it is dangerous for a monk to turn his eyes on her."

The Teaching of Ramakrishna

KALIPRASAD CHANDRA

When Kaliprasad Chandra met the Master, he could not make himself believe in the personal God. His future *guru* reassured him by pointing out to him that many others had gone through this same state of mind and that Naren, for example, wept as soon as he heard the names of Radha and Krishna. Soon the gods and goddesses who were seen in visions by him who was to become Swami Abhedananda disappeared, and it did not take him long to experience the void and the other attributes of impersonal *Brahman*.

SUBODH GHOSH

On the first visit by Subodh Ghosh, the future Swami Subodhananda, the priest of Kali greeted him with these words: "The Divine Mother tells me that you will succeed. Those whom she sends me are certain to attain to true spirituality." And so it was. The Revelation manifested itself suddenly in Subodh and his soul was flooded with joy.

❊

183

GIRISH CHANDRA GOSH

Among the adult believers around Sri Ramakrishna, one of the most striking seems to have been the talented actor and the most celebrated playwright of his time in Bengal, Girish Chandra Gosh. Having lost his faith in God when his wife died, he was leading a dissipated life and had abandoned himself to drunkenness when he first became acquainted with the priest of Kali, whose most rebellious disciple he was to prove to be. He had gone to Dakshineswar with the intention of insulting the man of God, and so he told him: "I get drunk in order to show what I think of your Lord." The Master replied calmly: "Then drink to God's health, for perhaps He too drinks." Girish shouted back in anger: "What do you know about it?" Ramakrishna countered: "If He did not drink, would the world be the wrong way round?" Then Sri Ramakrishna asked Girish whether he might not attend a play and visit his theater, and Girish issued an invitation. After the actor had gone, someone who had observed the exchange asked the Master, in connection with "that low character": "What do you see in him?" and the priest replied: "A great adorer of God."

A few days later Ramakrishna went to the theater and, after the performance, Girish, full of vanity, sought the approbation of his future *guru,* who con-

Girish Chandra Gosh

fined himself to saying: "You are suffering from a deformity of the soul." Girish asked how he could be cured of it, and Ramakrishna replied: "You are in great need of religion." In a rage, the actor shouted insults at the Master, who was unmoved and who, after a word of blessing, went away. There were several very painful encounters during which the adorer of the Divine Mother gave evidence of patience without limit and love without limit as well. The terrible drunkard finally became somewhat milder, though he did not want to submit to the slightest discipline of prayer. Ramakrishna thereupon asked him for "power of attorney" to perform in his stead the religious obligations of which Girish was in need. Disturbed, the actor

❈

agreed. The firm and clever influence of his *guru* completely changed the actor, who became one of the great spiritual forces who dedicated themselves to the Master with immeasurable ardor until his death.

With his last breath, according to those who were present, Girish murmured: "This madness of matter . . . hides God's face from me. Take away this veil from my eyes, O Ramakrishna." (*The Gospel of M.,* page 51.)

VIVEKANANDA

Narendra Nath Dutta, Sri Ramakrishna's favorite disciple, his beloved disciple, to whom, before he died, he gave complete initiation and his own seal, was to succeed his *guru* as the head of the other disciples. In order to spread the message that he had received through the entire world to greater effect, the priest of Kali needed an inspired propagandist who possessed at the same time the sacred fire and the power of the Word, the gift of language. Naren, the future Swami Vivekananda, had these gifts and many more besides. Long before he knew Naren, as in the case of Rakhal, his other favorite spiritual son, the priest of Dakshineswar had seen him in a vision in the guise of a wise man plunged in the meditation of the Absolute, having agreed to be incarnated in a human body in order to assist his Master in the earthly task of which at that time Naren was utterly ignorant.

Vivekananda (Narendra Nath Dutta)

Narendra was born in 1863 in Calcutta to an aristo-
cratic *kshatriya* family. His father, an outstanding
lawyer practicing in the High Court of Justice in
Calcutta, scorned religious and social conventions. His
very mystic mother was devoted to the great epics of
Indian history. From his childhood Naren impressed
those about him by his various qualities: physical

❧

187

beauty, keen intelligence, great courage, and love of truth and purity. This splendid aggregate of virtues was further augmented by broad knowledge in the fields of science and philosophy, a leaning toward music, and a profound taste for meditation. His forceful personality was enhanced by his stature and the fire of his eyes.

When Naren studied the nineteenth-century philosophers in his preparatory school, his childhood faith was shaken. He wanted to find a satisfactory explanation of God, a certitude. He soon discovered that universal reason was cold and lifeless. His ardent nature could not be satisfied with a mere abstraction. It demanded some external support, a *guru* who would sustain him in his hours of temptation and assuage the violent surges of his spirit. Drawn by the virtue, the integrity, and the ideal of Keshub Chandra Sen, he, like his friend, Rakhal, joined the *Brahmasamaj,* but he could find no *guru* there who could tell him that he had seen God.

One day he went to the garden-temple with Keshub and some young friends. He was eighteen years old. At Sri Ramakrishna's request he chanted a few hymns into which he put his entire soul. The adorer of the Divine Mother at once went into *samadhi.* When he regained consciousness, he led Naren to the veranda north of his bedroom. They were alone. Addressing the young man as if they were old friends, he said:

❁

Ah, you have come very late. Why have you made me
wait so long? My ears are weary of listening to futile
conversations. How I wished to pour my spirit into
the heart of someone ready to receive my message. (*The
Gospel of M.*, page 57.)

He was weeping as he spoke, and he urged Naren to
come to see him often. He told him that a great
mission awaited him: the alleviation of human suffering in his country.

Stunned and frightened, Naren wondered: "Why
did I come? The man is completely insane; how does
he dare to talk to me like this?" (*The Gospel of M.*,
page 57.) But, when he had gone into another room, he
understood, as he listened to the Master speaking to the
other visitors, that on the contrary he was in the
presence of a man of lofty spirit, logical, obviously
sincere—certain proof of the spirituality with which he
was credited.

Naren asked: "Have you seen God?" and the Master
replied:

Yes, I have seen Him as I see you. I have spoken to Him
more intimately than I am speaking to you. But, my
child, who then desires to see God? People shed floods
of tears for money, wives, and children. If they wept a
single day for God they would see Him. (*The Gospel of
M.*, page 57.)

Naren was moved. For the first time he was meeting
someone who had seen God. But he could not reconcile
the words that he had just heard with the scene that

❀

had taken place on the veranda. Deeply troubled, thinking that he was dealing with a lunatic, he returned to his home. Sri Ramakrishna's prophecy about him and his mission had offended him. He loathed soothsayers. But in spite of everything he was obsessed by the thought of the saint of Dakshineswar.

A month later, when he made his second visit, the young man had barely sat down beside the Master when he felt Ramakrishna's right foot touch him. The effect was instantaneous. Naren felt that he was losing consciousness. The walls and the furniture seemed to be spinning and dissolving round him, and he cried out in terror: "What are you doing to me?" He saw his own self and the universe disappearing into a nameless void. Sri Ramakrishna, laughing, reassured him. Naren thought that he had been hypnotized. He could not understand how a madman could succeed in casting a spell on anyone as strong as himself. He left in great confusion, more firmly resolved than ever to keep up his guard with this strange man.

The third visit went no better. A single move by the Master—a touch on his shoulder—was enough to cause Naren to lose consciousness completely. While he was in this state, Ramakrishna questioned him on his spiritual ancestors, his mission in this world, and the length of his earthly life. The replies that the Master received confirmed what he already thought. Among other things, he recognized that Naren was a sage who had attained to perfection and that, on the day when he should learn what his true nature was, he would abandon his body in *Yoga* by an act of will.

Further meetings purged Naren's mind of all suspicions concerning Sri Ramakrishna. The integrity, the purity, the lack of self-interest, the renunciation, and the remarkable spiritual power of this saint shone then before the eyes of the young student who could not resign himself to accepting an imperfect mortal as his *guru*. A human intermediary should not be required between himself and God. He laughed at Ramakrishna's visions, which he regarded as hallucinations. But in the secrecy of his heart he already felt a great love for this older man who had no attraction other than the radiance of the Invisible on his countenance.

Naren's doubts about him filled Ramakrishna with joy. He begged his disciple to test him further in order himself to be more certain of his own realizations. Sometimes he was wounded by Naren's biting criticisms and his harsh words. The Divine Mother consoled him: "Why do you listen to him? In a few days he will believe everything that you tell him." (*The Gospel of M.*, page 58.)

The *guru* wanted to draw his *chela* into the study of the nondualist *Vedanta*, the *advaita*. The pupil called it blasphemy to believe that man was One with his Creator. One day at the garden-temple the priest said to his young friend: "What stupidity it is to doubt! Everything that we see is God. This cup is God, and we too are God." (*The Gospel of M.*, page 58.) Then he

❊

191

touched Naren's arm. The boy lost consciousness and perceived that everything in the world was God. A new universe unfolded round him. When he returned to his home, he was stupefied to recognize that the food, the plates, the people, all were God. In the street he saw that the horses and carriages and houses were God.

He was so deeply rapt in his thoughts that his parents believed him ill. He remembered Ramakrishna's explanation: "The waves of the Ganges belong to the Ganges, but one wave is not the Ganges." (*The Gospel of M.,* page 812.) This quieted him somewhat after the violence of the shock produced by the discovery that *everything* was God, in God. He regained his equilibrium, having had the foretaste of the future experiences that would demonstrate the truth of the *Vedanta* to him.

At the beginning of 1884 Naren's father died suddenly. His family situation became uncertain. Unsuccessfully he looked for work. Bitterness invaded his being. Naren began to doubt the existence of God. In the face of the misery that confronted his family and himself, his pride revolted. There were unfounded, malicious rumors in circulation about him, troubling even some of his friends. They grieved him, but he was happy when he learned that Sri Ramakrishna, in contrast, had never doubted him. The crisis came. After a whole day without food, Naren arrived at his house, but he was too weak to go inside and rest his exhausted body. He sat down opposite the house, incapable of going farther. His mind was wandering. Suddenly he found the solution to the question that had long haunted him; the simultaneous existence of misery and divine justice, this presence of suffering in creation. His body reinvigorated, he fell serenely asleep. At last he knew that he had a vast spiritual task to accomplish. He resolved to renounce the world completely, and he went to ask the benediction of his *guru*. The priest of Kali, who knew everything, even before Naren opened his mouth, wept with joy.

His family's poverty having reached the extreme, Naren begged Ramakrishna to pray to the Divine Mother for some improvement in his financial situation. His *guru* replied that he would not disturb the Mother with so vulgar a request and that Naren should take care of the matter himself. The young man went into Kali's sanctuary. There he saw the Image like a living Goddess ready to grant him wisdom and liberation. He forgot the rest. The Master reproached him for this and made him go back into the temple to pray to the Divine Mother. Three times Naren went in, and three times he forgot his request. Then Ramakrishna promised him that his family would always have enough to live on.

This was a great experience for Naren, who understood that the Divine Power could not be ignored and that it was unavoidable for believers to have recourse to the personal god. Happy to see his disciple converted to the imperative need of the personal god, the adorer of

❁

the Mother seated himself beside Naren the next day, pointed him out to another of the devout, and said:

I see that I am he. I really feel no difference. A stick floating on the Ganges seems to cut the water into two parts, but in truth the water remains one. Do you understand my point of view? (*The Gospel of M.,* page 60.)

Later Naren was able to say:

Ramakrishna was the only person who believed in me throughout everything and never doubted; this was not true of either my mother or my brothers. It was his unshakable confidence and his unshakable love that bound me to him forever. He alone knew how much I loved him. (*The Gospel of M.,* page 60.)

The bare accounts of the external relations between the *guru* and his *chela* hardly make it possible to imagine the hours of serious intimacy and spiritual exchanges that sealed the extraordinary understanding between these two souls. The disciples themselves maintained silence about their personal experiences. So it was for Ramakrishna and Vivekananda. They let the world know only what the world was able to grasp, and the rest had to be left in mystery. A few days before his death, however, the Master summoned Naren and asked to be left alone with him. He contemplated him tenderly and then went into *samadhi.* Naren, too, lost consciousness, and, when he came to himself, Ramakrishna, who was weeping, said: "I have

The Divine Mother in the form of Anapurna, the generous

given you everything, I have nothing left." From that moment onward master and disciple were but one. It was time to start the work of Naren, of Ramakrishna-Vivekananda.

The priest of Kali had wanted his disciple to attain to the realization of the Self before he could devote himself profitably to the service of mankind. To this Vivekananda was to bring an energy of action and a

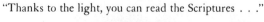
"Thanks to the light, you can read the Scriptures . . ."

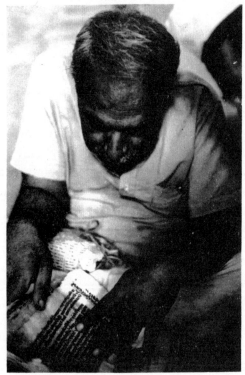

passion capable of surmounting all obstacles. His *guru* was not unaware of this, even though he was already in the other sphere, and this caused him to say:

The Absolute is without ties to good and evil. It is like the light of a lamp. Thanks to it, you can read the Holy Scriptures. But by the same light you can also forge signatures. Whatever the sin, the evil, or the misery that we find in the world, they are misery, evil, or sin only in relation to us. The Absolute is not affected by them. It is above and beyond. Its sun shines equally on the Evil and on the Good . . . I am afraid that you have to accept the facts of the universe as they are. It is not given to man to penetrate the ways of the Lord. . . . (*The Gospel of M.,* page 437.)

Silence

Contemplating this peace of supreme silence,
    that envelops those who know,
    those who possess knowledge
that is lofty and whole and firm,
    for to them there is no more lure
    in pursuit of the things of this world;
    contemplating
    this divine whole
that nothing excludes, in which all begins,
eternal, tranquil felicity,
    the serene freshness of true being;

    contemplating again and again
    the Eternal, Being in itself,

❈

witness to all and source of all, that leads
   to the ultimate purity
   of Wisdom,
those who pass beyond the three conditions,
so that they no more wake or sleep or dream;
   —looking on you, the unflawed flame
   of that light
   that dissolves
   the unknowing vision of the multiple,
ocean of bliss that even the six beliefs
   can never reach
   —and you, o peace;
   looking on you, great sea
   of joy,
   well-spring of all life,
   nectar of delight,
splendidly golden, jewel,
innermost essence of nonduality
that holds sovereign domain in me,
infinite radiance enveloping the world,
infinity alight with glory,
Joy—O Joy!

> (Poem of Thayuma navar,
> in *Studies on Ramana Maharshi,* ed. Adyar.)

Sannyasin in the Himalayas

❈

4

The Ramakrishna Mission

A few years after Sri Ramakrishna's death, Vivekananda went to Europe to carry the message of his Master. This first voyage was made in 1893 and was followed by a second in 1896, but before going to Europe he had traveled throughout India on a number of occasions. During his various lectures he always maintained, among other things, that the Indian Texts that were studied in the universities did not deal with a dead civilization, as some people in Europe tended to

❊

The Ramakrishna Mission

believe. These Texts are alive with the same life that filled them thousands of years ago, since the very beginning of time. Their truth stands unaltered. Vivekananda added that the coming of Ramakrishna, who had appeared in the normal course of history, was an event comparable to that of Jesus Christ for Christians and that it was an obligation on himself, as Ramakrishna's disciple, to make this revelation to the world.

This was his mission. It was begun with the establishment of the *Math* of Belur, the sanctuary that sheltered a dozen of the Master's disciples under Vivekananda's leadership. This new order of monks (each of whom took the vow of the *sannyasin* and chose a new monastic name) set as its ideal the combination of religious meditation with the study of the sciences while at the same time dedicating itself to the "service" of mankind, as the Master had counseled its members.

Ever since, the Ramakrishna Mission has continued to be an effective force in India and the whole world, but its history is too much for the framework of this little book. It should be added, however, as far as France is concerned, that Swami Siddheswarananda, who was ordained a monk of the Order of Ramakrishna at the *Math* of Belur by Swami Brahmananda, a disciple of Ramakrishna, went to France in 1937. The Swamis of the Order of Ramakrishna never force themselves on anyone and go only when and where they are invited. When various groups of persons inter-

ested in Eastern thought want a more direct contact, a Swami brings them the traditional teachings of India.

Such was the case with Swami Siddheswarananda, who founded the *Ashram* at Gretz and directed it until his death on April 2, 1957. *A great number of persons knew him and loved him; many venerated him.*

The radiant influence of this Vedantic Center is practiced through disciples, studies, and lectures attended by faithful friends and a large public. The Center publishes a periodical, *Vedanta,* which contains articles on India's philosophy and spirituality.

In India, similarly, Ramakrishna's work is furthered through the Ramakrishna *Math* and the Ramakrishna Mission. It was a new and dynamic message that modern India heard when Swami Vivekananda proclaimed, in his Master's name, that "renunciation accompanied by social assistance should be the national ideal of India."

In order to fulfill this ideal in a concrete fashion, Vivekananda founded the Movement that bears the holy name of Sri Ramakrishna, the prophet of harmony among all religions. This Movement includes two branches: the Ramakrishna *Math* and the Ramakrishna Mission, both known throughout the entire world for their philanthropic endeavors.

After their Master's death, the disciples wandered

A monk of the Ramakrishna Mission saying his prayers to "Mother Ganges" (Uttarkashi, Himalayas)

❁

hither and thither, guided by the need for their help in various regions, devoting themselves to social-service undertakings, while Swami Ramakrishnananda (Sashi) remained as the custodian of the relics at the *Math,* which he never left and of which he remained the faithful guardian until his death. In 1897 part of the Ramakrishna Mission was enlisted in action to combat famine and malaria, and a year later it joined the fight on pestilence.

The monks' aspiration was still greater. More than an effective charitable endeavor, they sought the practical realization of their Master's religious message in the nation's life. Indeed, they hoped to see it develop on the level of international exchanges in order to lay the groundwork for understanding of all contemporary religious and intellectual problems on a world-wide basis, a synthesis of the thinking of East and West.

But Vivekananda knew that the social conditions of India fell far short of the ideal preached by his religion and that the *Vedanta,* which awakens and illuminates the individual consciousness, had not yet succeeded in permeating the nation's life. He believed that, in order to become an effective force, religion and philosophy should be closely united and—in some way—socialized in order to provide the basis for all the activities that he envisaged. These activities should be imbued with the fundamental concept that every individual, independently of his caste, his religion, or his race, ought to be regarded as a manifestation of the Divine: "Who can offer pity to his fellow? Not pity but service."

Swami Siddheswarananda at the *ashram* of Gretz

Founded a short time after the Master's death, the
Ramakrishna *Math,* the purpose of which was monastic training, now has 144 centers spread throughout
the entire world. Even while in their monasteries the
monks lead a life of spiritual and intellectual disciplines, they remain in contact with the environment
around them. The major *Math,* the center for all the
others, is situated at Belur, in the vicinity of Calcutta

❊

and on the shore of the Ganges. It carries on its cultural activities by means of lectures, publications, classes, reading rooms, and bookshops, as well as the celebration of religious festivals in a chapel open to all.

The Calcutta Cultural Institute, founded in 1938, seeks to apply the religious ideal of India to contemporary life. It organizes international congresses to which Indian and foreign scholars are invited for the exchange of views in the intellectual, philosophical, religious, and social fields.

Well aware that education is one of the nation's vital needs, the Ramakrishna Mission directs a large part of its effort toward this end. It establishes schools in which the curriculum is based on the study programs of the government institutions, but it does not overlook physical culture, which is directed by monks specializing in the field. Other monks run orphanages, industrial and technical schools, and, of course, numerous *ashrams,* for the primary place is always reserved for religion, since the mastery of the soul is indispensable to the development of the body.

"What our country needs today is muscles of iron and nerves of steel," Vivekananda counseled. "What we need is a religion that creates men, what we need is theories that create men, what we need is general education."

The principal monastery of the Order of Ramakrishna in southern India is near Madras. There the Sri Ramakrishna Mission runs a high school for boys, divided into three branches based on the students' aptitudes. Established in 1932, this school had only 180 pupils in its first year. In 1953 it had 4,363. New buildings, including an enclosed gymnasium, a stadium, and a library, have been erected.

Various centers also have evening classes and courses in Sanskrit. The girls' schools, the internal organization of which is comparable to that of the boys' schools, are augmented by special branches that prepare girls to become nurses and midwives. They have even added extra classes in music, drawing, and domestic science, without overlooking sewing and gardening.

In addition to the establishment of these various schools, institutions, and hospitals, it should be added that the Order has founded missions in other countries (East Pakistan, Burma, Ceylon, Malaysia, England, France, the United States, etc.) with a view to presenting the true image of contemporary Indian culture and realizing the ideal preached in Ramakrishna's name by Vivekananda.

Emblem of the Ramakrishna Mission

5

The Message of

Ramakrishna

. . . I have had the good fortune to sit at the feet of him whose life, a thousand times more than his teaching, was a living commentary on the texts of the *Upanishads* incarnated in the human form, the harmony of all the varied ideas of India . . . India has been rich in thinkers and wise men. One had a tremendous brain, another had an immense heart. The times were ripe for the birth of him who in the same body would have the brilliant intellect of Sankara and the wondrous heart of Chaitanya, him who would see the same spirit at work

❋

in every faith, the same God—him who would see the Divine in every creature—him whose heart would weep for all the poor, the weak, the outcast, the oppressed, all those who are in India and all those who are outside of India—him who would be the realization of universal harmony, the religion of reason and love. . . . This man was born . . . in a city more Europeanized than any other in India. There he lived without any learning drawn from books. This inspired intelligence could barely write his own name. But the most eminent graduates of our University recognized a giant of the mind in him. (Lecture by Vivekananda in Calcutta on *The Vedanta in All Its Aspects,* quoted in Rolland, *Life of Ramakrishna,* page 289.)

There could be no better introduction to this concluding section than the quotation of this evaluation that comes from Ramakrishna's chief disciple. In eloquent fashion it illustrates the reverberations that the great mystic's message has made in India.

Many of his compatriots believe that, by offering them a new way of thinking and living, the priest of Kali infused Indian civilization with a renewed energy. To those who reproached Hinduism for creating a block to India's economic development he replied that this block resulted rather from faulty understanding of Hinduism, and he exerted every effort to make this religion known and extended in its highest form by freeing it of the excess of ritual that occasionally stifled it.

In these circumstances it is not surprising that he has

❀

left behind him a phalanx of disciples who have continued his apostolate and given it life in religious, philosophical, and social endeavors whose range is great. But the essence of the legacy bequeathed to mankind by the saint of Dakshineswar is not to be found here. It lies entirely on the level of God, or at the very least on the level of ideas for attaining to God. Its range is not geographically limited to India, any more than from the religious point of view it is confined to Hinduism. That is what enhances its worth to us.

In principle I have avoided making comparisons between the religious thinking of Sri Ramakrishna and that of Christianity in this little book. I have sought only, as my modest contribution to the already large number of biographies of the great Hindu Sage, to sketch the broad outlines of his spiritual experiences and recount the important events of his life, as well as his most significant works and deeds, without appending any personal commentaries.

In truth the mystic experience, in whatever form it takes, is beyond all measurement and all comparison and is always indescribable. "In the state of *samadhi,* reasoning ceases and man becomes mute. He has no power to describe what the Absolute is," the priest of Kali said. (*The Gospel of M.,* page 102.) A kind of aspiration toward the Absolute, the mystic experience goes beyond the reasonable limits of religion—it states without proving (this is the Christian point of view)— in order to grant unchallenged sovereignty to intuition,

❁

the inner voice. A phenomenon beyond the range of analysis, it is enveloped in mystery. It is a mystery. Whence its name. How can one judge a mystery?

But it is even more difficult to compare the religions of East and West; the words that are used never have quite the same meanings. They are "values" that are no more measurable one against another than are mystic experiences. One is dealing here with religious concepts that are different in essence and with phenomena that take place in a different atmosphere. It would be impossible to equate these spiritual experiences without taking the risk of changing their true meaning.

While the study of the Oriental religions discloses—to Christian eyes—certain harmonies of doctrine among them, doctrines that undoubtedly arose out of the same font of primordial truths of which India received the Revelation at the dawn of the ages, these similarities are also to be explained by a mental kinship that exists among the Asian races, so remote and so different from our Western races.

It must be added as well, and the synthesized description of Hinduism at the start of this book attests to the fact, that the Hindu religion presents a character that is at once complex and *mobile*. It is composed of a cluster of related religions that represent modalities of the Vedic tradition, the original source of all these sects, which, furthermore, are only developments of the same doctrine in various directions according to certain "points of view" in no way incompatible with one

❈

another. The word *darçana,* let us remember, which means *point of view,* in fact denotes the six great orthodox philosophical systems of the *Sanatana-Dharma.*

To this mobile aspect of the Hindu religion the personality of Sri Ramakrishna adds further difficulties. The peculiarities of his behavior result from the fact that he lived constantly on the threshold between the Absolute and the relative, and this led even his closest disciple astray. Now it must be pointed out that as a rule it was as the result of a sudden illumination that the lives of most of the Western mystics were finally fixed on God, in silence or in apostolate, in accordance with the message delivered by the personal Revelation of their own religions; whereas the adorer of Kali accepted all the new spiritual experiences that were offered to him and, if necessary, he went in search of them. He refused none of them, looking on each as an enrichment that complemented the others, and in each experience he attained to the supreme peak of *samadhi,* total fusion with the Divine.

In the face of so elusive a spirit how could one dare to frame a comparative judgment on the basis of Christian postulates without distorting every perspective and without the fear of committing unavoidable errors made all the more serious by reason of the fact that they concern religious consciousness and holiness? Here one is truly confronted with an exceptional case that must be described with respect in spite of the impossibility of filling in each of its details. The part played by mystery in Ramakrishna's life is undeniable to a Christian mind. But the attraction exercised by this saint is so strong, the intensity of his radiance is so profound, that we should like to try to identify the message that he left to the world in its universal sense, once we have attempted, as I have done here, to show what it is that prevents us from understanding it better.

Is not Ramakrishna's life, in which so many spiritual experiences were accumulated one after another, first of all a new and living teaching, a unique example? Does not his call to the harmony of all religions represent a major point in his message? To stimulate every soul to search for God, as he constantly did, seemed to him to be the first duty of the believer, but this quest must bring men together instead of dividing them. To him all religions were true in their essence, each providing a road of access to the Divine.

> No one of them possesses any right to universality, each being a message handed down at a certain epoch, to a given people. If one wanted to apply the commandments of a single revelation to all human societies, one would subject races that have nothing in common among themselves to concepts the full worth of which they would be incapable of grasping. (Swami Siddheswarananda, *Sri Ramakrishna and the Harmony of Religions*, page 4.)

The saint of Dakshineswar has demonstrated that

❊

inspiration comes from God alone, from His Grace, and that exclusive importance must not be attached to any religion to the detriment of the others. This initiative in mutual understanding, in tolerance, is a specifically Indian characteristic, but it did not prevent Ramakrishna from fulfilling his religious obligations in the strict Brahmin observance. He practiced other doctrines in order to understand them, to experience them, without *enlisting himself* in any, and he counseled his intimates to follow his example.

He labored ardently for the reconciliation of all religions, for their harmony, regarding this as being part of his mission. He did not attempt to resolve the contradictions that the Holy Books or the dogmas of various doctrines present among themselves. More concerned with the believer's genuine yearning for God than with the meticulous performance of ritual, he strove to bring about the awakening of souls and to teach them to seek God.

But there is a certain misunderstanding today in connection with Ramakrishna's researches in the structures of religions other than his own. It is so difficult to liberate oneself completely from certain widely accepted ideas that are only partly correct as to the relations that exist among the various religions. Undoubtedly no one has himself had sufficient experience.

The true lesson of the great mystic—it would seem—deals, rather than with the so-called "unity" of religions (an idea dear to Shuon and many others), with the *complementariness* of the various experiences that are connected with each. Ramakrishna was perhaps the first in our age to understand and live the previously dissociated and dual activity that consists, on the one hand, of abandoning creation (detachment) in order to find God, and, on the other, of fulfilling creation to the very end, equally in order to find God. Would it not be more accurate to speak of the "disengagement" of *advaita* and Buddhism, on the one hand, and, on the other, of the dynamic manifestation as it is presented by Christianity, Judaism, and Islam? Then these two poles are no longer mutually exclusive; instead, they form a perfect organic movement. Would this be the secret of eternal life and the way that leads to it according to the saint of Dakshineswar? Such a view dissolves all opposition, all arbitrary preference. God hides Himself and shows Himself, everything is secret and then everything bursts out into broad daylight. The man who succeeds in giving free play within himself to this double rhythm, who feels that he is at the same time a Person and the Impersonal, enjoys absolutely total freedom. He knows that he can neither find himself without losing himself nor lose himself without finding himself again. This interpretation—a mere suggestion—of one aspect of Sri Ramakrishna's thinking comes to mind when one reads his conversations on the bank of the Ganges when he allowed his exceedingly great thought to fly off into the Infinite

❈

with all the spiritual riches accumulated in him, and yet without abandoning his anchor point, the Divine Mother.

Therefore he never entertained the thought of creating a new religion. Quite the opposite. He prayed to Kali to save him from this: "Spare me the honor of forming adepts, do not found any religion through me as intermediary." On many occasions he asserted:

As many lights shine as there are pious pilgrims. If God is infinite, the ways that lead to Him must be infinite. . . . Why discuss or debate? What matters is to find God at all costs and not to torture oneself over the choice of the best road to take. Rigid adherence to certain dogmas is not indispensable; at times it can be harmful. If you know God, you will not concern yourself with doctrines. You could have read all the Holy Books of all the religions, you could believe in all the revealed credos, and yet be incapable of finding God! (*The Gospel of M.*)

Nor did Ramakrishna ever make the slightest effort at proselytization. He said: "Be like the flower: blossom freely and let the bees unburden your heart. Be the enchantment of the world, but hold no one prisoner to the beauty of your soul." (*The Gospel of M.*, page 103.) He urged his disciples to create no "Ramakrishna-ism" after his death and to launch no sectarianism. There should be no borders between men: "A river ought to flow freely, without dams. If it is stopped, it turns stagnant and becomes poisoned." (*The Gospel of M.*, page 103.)

❁

The priest of Kali, who liked to make abstractions of religious forms—even while he remained faithful to them—believed that the intelligence ought to be able to decide what choice should be made in every circumstance. He constantly emphasized the importance of *discrimination* to his disciples. But this quality presupposed a great strength in his spirit, because the higher intelligence (*boddhi*) is incompatible with a weak and fearful spirit. In this connection Vivekananda cited the example of Naciketas, the hero of the *Katha-Upanishad*; the young man who was so audacious that he did not hesitate to visit the god of death in order to rob him of his secret!

Ramakrishna combined this strength of intelligence with a remarkable flexibility. Swami Siddheswarananda recalled in this respect how in a few moments his Master's mind could assume a number of different and seemingly opposing positions. He believed, indeed, that the malleability of his mind was such that only a great artist could appreciate it. "Expansion is life, contraction is death," Vivekananda said. Now the power of expansion, the capacity to be but One with the other, represents the secret of the mystical experience. . . . From his youth, almost from his childhood, as we have seen, Ramakrishna possessed this very rare gift of being able to identify himself completely with others—on the material level by finding in his own body the physical characteristics of the man of whom he was thinking, and on the spiritual level by being united with him in the very core of being.

❁

It was the mystic paths that enabled the great Hindu saint to make these amazing identifications. Mysticism seemed to him the most natural of religious forms, the form whose attraction moved many spirits, because it fulfilled that need to believe "in something greater than oneself," to be fused in it in a state of consciousness superior to the waking state, a state that leads to ecstasy, to a form of ecstasy (there are many, just as there are many kinds of *samadhi*). Ecstasy, perhaps, could be defined as the consciousness of an unknown universe that is awakened while the awareness of the ordinary universe is asleep. This passionate desire to attain to God is part of every religion in the world. Is it not a bond, a universal language? So Ramakrishna thought. Throughout his life this was expressed in his teaching.

One conclusion, he declared, is forced on all believers: that of living in the *constant presence of God*. The worshiper of the Divine Mother did not hesitate to say that this was a supreme commandment taught to the faithful of all religions. Living in the presence of God represented permanent reality to him, and it ought to relegate the external practices of all religions to a secondary level. There is no more salutary method of destroying the "old being" in oneself in order to make possible the birth of what is really divine in all men. "This undertaking is not beyond our powers; that is what is proclaimed by the lives of the saints and

❁

sages of all religions." (Swami Siddheswarananda, *Harmony of Religions,* page 19.)

In Ramakrishna this fusion in God produced a complete effacement of self. In every being he saw the sovereign God and served him as such. To charity and philanthropy—ideas with which he seemed to associate a certain condescension—he preferred the love of his fellowman, which to him was only another form of adoration of God. "Real charity," he said, "is the love of God in all men."

All the life and teaching of the little Bengali peasant who became "the madman of God" lead us back to this adoration, to *Bhakti*. Some have regarded Ramakrishna as a Divine Incarnation, others as a saint. It makes no difference. What should inspire us with a fervor-filled respect for him is his tremendous love of God, a reflection of God's own love.

Deliberate withdrawal, lack of altruism, any selfish way of thinking or living were in his eyes simply a sign of separation from mankind, another obstacle to spiritual growth. The slightest effort toward active, effective solidarity represented to him a step toward Unity, the reincorporation of everything into God. This endless chain of souls of good will, invisible but real, furthers the slow but certain ascent of mankind so that it cannot tumble into the void.

Love alone can gather and unite the innumerable tiny human particles, immortal and born of God, that find their true reason for being and their ineluctable end only in Unity in God. The miraculous spiritual radiance of Sri Ramakrishna contributes and will always contribute to the friendship of men of East and West because it is by the gift of self, the love that unifies, *Bhakti,* that the supreme communion among souls is established.

Glossary

Advaita	Doctrine of the One without a second; monism
Ashram	Community; hermitage
Atman	The Supreme Being. *Brahman*. The Self that lives in each person
Avatar	The "Descent" of the Divine. The Divine Incarnation
Bhagavad-Gita	*The Song of the Blessed*. A religious and philosophical poem that is part of the Holy Scriptures
Bhakta	The practitioner of *Bhakti*, the aspirant who follows the path of devotion
Bhakti	Intense devotion
Brahma	One of the three gods in the Hindu Trinity
Brahman	The absolutely conditionless Being, pure Existence, Totality, the Absolute
Brahmin	A Hindu priest. The highest caste in India, possessing spiritual power
Brahmasamaj	A religious reform movement to restore the pure spirit of the *Vedas* in 1828
Chela	Disciple of a *guru*. One who follows a master's teaching
Darçana	Philosophical systems. Conceptions that start from a common origin, the *Veda*
Dharma	Law of a moral nature. Individual duty. What binds the individual to social life
Gunas	Attributes or qualities. They are three, characterizing the primordial substance
Guru	Spiritual instructor
Ishta	Image or form of the divinity chosen as the object of adoration

❁

Illustrations from the *Markandeya-Purana*

Isvara	Generic name for the unique and supreme God above the Trinity
Jivan-Mukti	He who lives released
Jnana-Yoga	Path to divine realization through intellectual knowledge
Kali	The Divine Mother
Karma	Law of retribution
Kirtan	Sacred song
Krishna	One of the great Divine Incarnations
Kshatriya	The second social caste, that of the warriors
Mahabharata	A great epic poem of which the *Bhagavad-Gita* is only a fragment
Mahabhava	Supreme rapture
Mantra	Formula for prayer
Math	Monastery

Maya	The manifest as it appears to us. The force of illusion and one of the names of the Divine Mother
Nirvikalpa-Samadhi	The highest state of *samadhi*
Pandit	A scholar, learned in sacred subjects
Parias	Those who belong to no caste—"casteless" or "untouchables"
Puranas	Historical and mythological narratives linked to sacred tradition
Rama	One of the great Divine Incarnations
Ramayana	A great epic poem
Rig-Veda	The most ancient of the four *Vedas*
Rishis	Great sages to whom Truth has been revealed
Sadhana	Asceticism, spiritual discipline
Sadhu	Monk
Sakti (Shakti)	Goddess symbolizing the God's power and energy, the Divine Mother, *Maya*

Samadhi	State of ecstatic union with God
Samsara	Sequence of successive existences. The phenomenal world
Sanatana-Dharma	Eternal or universal *dharma*. True name of the religious tradition
Sannyasin	An ascetic who practices absolute renunciation
Satchitananda	A formula meaning pure existence, pure intelligence, pure felicity: *Brahman*
Siva (Shiva)	One of the gods in the Hindu Trinity, the destructive aspect of the Divine
Sri	A title of respect: Lord
Sruti	Revelation received by the *Rishis*. The Sacred Scriptures
Sudras	The fourth of the Indian castes. Laborers of all kinds
Swami	A spiritual master
Tantras	Texts connected with the religious sect called Tantrism
Trimurti	Hinduism's religious Trinity
Upanishads	Religious and philosophical treatises forming the last part of the Revelation
Vaishnavas	Believers who practice the worship of Vishnu
Vaishyas	Third caste in India. The middle class and merchants
Veda	Knowledge in its highest form, Sacred Knowledge; the collection of the revealed Scriptures
Vedanta	The end of the *Vedas: Veda* and *Vedanta* together form the *sruti*
Vedism	Collectively, everything connected with the *Veda*
Vishnu	One of the gods of the Hindu Trinity. The preserving aspect of the Divine
Yoga	One of the six great philosophical systems of India. One of the classic roads by which to attain to union with the ideal

Chronology

The Hindus having always shown great disinterest in matters of history and chronology, it is difficult to establish precise dates for the ancient periods of Indian history.

Prehistoric Period

The origins of *Brahmanism*, of the Vedic Revelation, and of the creation of a Brahmin religious and social state, with its rites and castes, are lost in prehistoric obscurity. No dates are known for the actual written appearance of the *Vedas*. In chronological order there were: the *Vedas*, the *Upanishads*, the *Great Epic*, and all the Books that derive from them.

556 B.C.	Birth of Buddha
540	Birth of Jina
520	Death of Lao-Tseu
519	Sermon of Benares
489	Death of Confucius

The Beginning of the Historic Period

It started with the first dynasty, that of the Mauryas, from the fourth to the second centuries B.C. In 327 B.C. India was invaded by

227

Alexander the Great. The most powerful sovereign, Asoka, was converted to Buddhism in 260 B.C.

The Sunga Dynasty began about 175 B.C. King Menander (Milinda) reigned in the Punjab and concerned himself with philosophical problems. An Indo-Greek monarchy established a foothold in Gandhara. This was the period of Greek-Buddhist art.

The Kushana Dynasty—first to third centuries A.D.	160	Nagarjuna
King Kanishka was the protector of the Buddhist communities		
Gupta Dynasty—beginning in 320 A.D.		Bodhidharma Zen Buddhism
Accession of Sandragupta I. The monarchs proclaimed themselves "great adorers of the Lord"	622	Muhammad's Hegira to Medina
and adepts of the cult of Vishnu	642	Arab victory over Persia at Nehavend
	661–750	Omeyad Dynasty in Damascus

The So-Called *Rajput* Period

From the eighth to the tenth centuries A.D. under local monarchies. Decline of Buddhism in India		
Eighth-ninth century: Sankara—nondualist *Vedanta* (*advaita*)	787	Council of Nicea
Ninth century: Spread of *Bhakti*	800	Coronation of Charlemagne

Episodes from the *Ramayana* (Temple pillar, Pattadakal)

	922	Execution of Al-Hallaj in Bagdad
Eleventh century: Ramanuja (died in 1137). Vishnuism	1099	First Crusade Capture of Jerusalem
Twelfth century: Muslim conquest	1187	Saladin's recapture of Jerusalem.
	1209	St. Francis of Assisi founds his Order
Fourteenth century: Turkish-Afghan monarchy in Delhi	1453	Constantinople taken by the Turks

The Great Moguls

	1530	Death of Baber, founder of the Great Mogul's empire in India
Emperor Akbar, a sovereign inspired by a great spirit of tolerance. He granted equal rights to Hindus and Muslims		
Established in India, Islam in no way hampered the power of Hinduism and its religious and literary development	1603	Tokugawa in Japan. Decline of Buddhism
Eighteenth century: preservation of religious tendencies in existing sects. Slight outside and foreign influences	1642–3	Fifth Dalai Lama becomes Priest-King of Tibet. Construction of the Potala at Lhassa

Contemporary Hinduism

Contemporary Hinduism represented by strong personalities	1769	Shinto becomes Japan's state reli-

whose influence extended to the West

Ram Mohun Roy (born in 1774) founder of Unitarianism, which was to become *Brahmasamaj*

Keshub Chandra Sen (born in 1838) continued *Brahmasamaj* and caused the schism in this Movement. He founded the *Nava Vishana*, or New Dispensation

Dayananda Sarasvati (1824–83). Started a reaction against *Brahmasamaj* in order to return to the genuine Vedic tradition by founding the *Aryasamaj*

Ramakrishna (1836–86). Great saint, regarded as an Incarnation, faithful to the teaching of Sankara's *Vedanta* while at the same time experimenting with the mystic paths of other religions

Vivekananda (1862–1902). Disciple of Ramakrishna, propagated his teaching and founded the monastic Order of Ramakrishna, then the Ramakrishna Mission attached to the Order, thus establishing philanthropic centers in India and abroad (headquarters in Belur)

Ramana Maharshi (died in 1950). His mystic experience assumed an extraordinary character

Sri Aurobindo Ghose (1872–1951). A great thinker and writer who became a great mystic devoted wholly to spiritual realization

gion. Nepal adheres to Hinduism

1890   Revival of Buddhism in Japan

Bibliography

Ashrama, Advaita. *Ramakrishna: A Biography in Pictures.* Vendata Press 1974

Aurobindo, Sri. *La Bhagavad Gita, Commentaires.* Adrien Maisonneuve.

Aurobindo, Sri. "Le Secret du Veda." In Documents spirituels. Cahiera du Sud.

Chatterji, Usha. *Comment Comprendre la religion Hindoue.* Oliver Perrin.

French, Harold. *The Swan's Wide Waters: Ramakrishna and Western Culture.* Kennikat Press, 1974.

Grousset. *Les Philosophies Indiennes.* Desclée de Brouwer.

Isherwood, Christopher. *Ramakrishna and His Disciples.* Vendata Press, 1976.

Lemaitre, Solange. *L'Hindouisme ou Sanatana-Dharma.* Frayard.

Menen. *The New Mystics and the True Indian Tradition.* Thames and Hudson, 1974.

Mookerjee, Nanda, ed. *Sri Ramakrishna in the Eyes of Brahma and Christian Admirers.* South Asia Books, 1976.

Renou, Louis, translator. *Anthologie Sanskrit.* Payot, 1947.

Renou, Louis, translator. *Hymnes et Priéres du Veda.* Translated from Sanskrit. Adrien Maisonneuve, 1938.

Renou, Louis. *L'Hindousime.* Presses Universitaires de France.

श्रीमहाभारतं

श्रीमन्महर्षिवेदव्यासविरचिता

श्रीमन्महाभारतसंहिता ।

—◆◆◆—

आदि सभा वन पर्व्वघटितः ।

———

प्रथमखण्डः ।

—◆—

साधारणविद्यावृद्ध्यर्थकश्रीयुक्तसमाजाधिपतीनामनुमत्यनुसारेण

तत्समभीयपण्डितैः संशोधितः ।

—•+•—

कलिकाताराजधान्यां ।

इदुक्रेश्नाख्यमुद्रायन्त्रालये ।

मुद्रितः ।

———

प्रकाब्दाः १७५६ ।

Renou, Louis, translator. *Les Upanishads*. Adrien Maisonneuve.

Schure, Edouard. *The Ancient Mysteries of the East: Ramakrishna*. Rudolf Steiner Publications, 1971.

Stark, Claude Alan. *God of All: Sri Ramakrishna's Approach to Religious Purity*. Cape Cod, 1974.

Stroup, Herbert Hewitt. *Like A Great River; An Introduction to Hinduism*. Harper and Row, 1972.

Vivekananka, Swami. *Ramakrishna and His Message*. Vendata Press, 1971.

Yogeshananda, Swami, compiled by. *The Visions of Sri Ramakrishna*. Vendata Press, 1976.

❀

Acknowledgments
for Illustrations

Musée Guimet, pp. ii, xviii, 12, 17, 24, 25, 28, 34–35, 63, 87, 92, 94, 141, 194, 224, 225

Louis Frédéric-Rapho, pp. 6–7, 10, 15, 27, 38, 40, 48, 51, 58–59, 90–91, 107, 113, 116, 144, 198, 202, 205, 229

Denis Brihat-Rapho, pp. xiii, 168, 196, 218–19

Centre Védantique Râmakrishna, Gretz, pp. xi, 45, 68, 120, 123, 129, 156–57, 158, 172, 175

Éditions du Seuil, pp. viii, 207, 233. Page viii reproduces the Sanskrit text of the *Katha-Upanishad*, vi, 3–15

Talwar-Viollet, p. 64

Premier album de mythologie hindoue, by Jean Herbert and H. Ghaffar (Éditions Derain, Lyons), p. 73

The Archeology of World Religions, by Jack Finegan (Princeton University Press), p. 22 (photographed from the University of Pennsylvania Museum)

The Gospel of Ramakrishna, by M., translated from Bengali into English and with an introduction by Swami Nikhilananda (Ramakrishna-Vivekananda Center, New York), pp. 44, 53, 54, 67, 81, 104, 128, 135, 147, 160, 171, 177, 181, 185, 187

❊

Illustration from the *Markandeya-Purana*

A Rajput painting: Parvarti on
the tiger (eighteenth century)

Index

❀

Index

239

INDEX

240

INDEX

INDEX

❀